Palgrave Studies in Third Sector Research

This book series focuses on the third sector— the sphere of society that is distinct from the family, the market economy, and political power/the state. The third sector has been historically institutionalized in different ways across countries and is subject to different scholarly traditions. Palgrave Studies in Third Sector Research addresses contemporary themes related to this societal sphere and its components.

This series has three main editorial aims; the first is to facilitate the dialogue across institutional contexts and scholarly perspectives, and will therefore publish studies of the third sector, the social and solidary economy, civil society, voluntary sector, non-profit sector, philanthropic sector and other related concepts. The second aim of the series is to publish contributions from all the regions of the world, including the Global South, and to foster comparisons across countries and global regions. The third aim of the series is to stimulate new thematic, theoretical and methodological developments related to both long-standing scholarly and emergent themes.

Mary-Beth Raddon

The Business of Hope

Professional Fundraising in Neoliberal Canada

palgrave
macmillan

Mary-Beth Raddon
Department of Sociology
Brock University
St. Catharines, ON, Canada

ISSN 2662-690X ISSN 2662-6918 (electronic)
Palgrave Studies in Third Sector Research
ISBN 978-3-031-18836-7 ISBN 978-3-031-18837-4 (eBook)
https://doi.org/10.1007/978-3-031-18837-4

This Palgrave Macmillan imprint is published by the registered company Springer Nature Switzerland AG.
The registered company address is: Gewerbestrasse 11, 6330 Cham, Switzerland

To Mum, with love and gratitude.

Preface

As a sociologist, I am fascinated with research that explores the relationship of structure, agency, and power in contemporary social change. How do we make the social world? How does the social world make us? For Canadians of my generation coming of age in the 1980s, the ascendance of neoliberal capitalism altered the world as we knew it and remains the change movement I grapple with. Neoliberalism is the term academics give to the political movement that gained electoral power in many Western states in the 1980s with a mission to reform welfare states along market lines. Neoliberalism, however, is more than a set of pro-market policies for generating a more business-friendly political economy. More than "capitalism on steroids," neoliberalism is also a governing rationality, a pervasive way of perceiving and valuing all dimensions of life, ourselves included, in economic terms—especially along the model of financial markets—as entrepreneurial, value-maximizing units of competitive human capital.

Describing and accounting for sweeping political and cultural change is challenging. In this book, I come at it by shining a light on the practices and perspectives of an extraordinary middle-class occupational group. Fundraising as an expert occupation in Canada owes itself to neoliberal policy change through which nonprofit and voluntary sector institutions became more dependent on private charity and philanthropy for basic operations. Neoliberalization also enriched Canada's business elite. The new heights of accumulation, coupled with a nonprofit sector in perpetual need of private donations, opened careers for professional fundraisers.

Fundraisers became brokers between a limited number of wealthy families—the beneficiaries of neoliberalism's upward redistribution of wealth—and the nonprofit organizations that benefit, in turn, from these families' largess. Fundraisers advance organizations' social mission by making a convincing case for a share of donor wealth, appealing to donors' generosity, as well as their reputational and personal interests. Basically, the fundraisers' job is to match the philanthropic aspirations of wealthy individuals and families with the need for private donations, often on painstakingly negotiated terms.

In *No Such Thing as a Free Gift: The Gates Foundation and the Price of Philanthropy*, Linsey McGoey (2015) compares gilded age philanthropy to its present-day variant, philanthrocapitalism. Whereas all philanthropy legitimizes extreme wealth, McGoey argues that social acceptance of modern mega-philanthropy is new. My research provides a partial explanation for the adulation philanthropists enjoy in contemporary culture. Fundraisers not only serve as intermediaries between the super-rich and the organizations to which they donate, they also communicate to the wider public. Their work helps ensure that donors receive positive recognition, that their gifts are met with gratitude, not cynicism, and that their reputations are enhanced. This book explores how fundraisers understand that work and how these understandings accord with the theory of neoliberalism as a governing rationality.

The period this research addresses is approximately the late 1980s to the global financial crisis of 2008. In late 2008 and early 2009, I interviewed 50 experienced fundraisers from across Canada, asking them to reflect on their careers and discuss changes they have observed in the profession of fundraising in Canada. The timing of the interviews coincided with the global financial crisis and recession, which was fortuitous for what it revealed. Fundraisers' careers to that point had flourished as the nonprofit and voluntary sector responded to state restructuring, particularly with the introduction of competitive proposal funding that left organizations with precarious or insufficient funding for key activities. Major gift fundraising was the fastest growing fundraising strategy, primarily benefitting universities, hospital foundations, and large cultural institutions. New tax rules led to massive increases in the number and magnitude of large donations. However, the 2008 financial crisis interrupted this heyday and introduced a moment of doubt about the trajectory of major gift fundraising, which had been driving growth in the fundraising industry.

As I was travelling to Canadian cities to conduct interviews, the financial crisis was foiling fundraising goals and forecasts. One fundraiser was unemployed at the time of his interview because his position had been terminated. To observers like me, the recession cast a shadow of uncertainty over the fundraising enterprise. Yet the fundraisers I met were an upbeat lot. When asked about the impact of the recession, they spoke of the need to be more innovative and enterprising in raising money, to operate their fundraising shops more efficiently, and to continue making charitable giving more tax-favourable to those with capital assets. Gordon, the director of an international fundraising firm with 25 years' fundraising experience, stated: "The recession has affected those organizations who use the recession as an excuse to stop asking for money."

Such talk exemplified what is meant by neoliberal rationality. Scarcity of funding was societally defined as the problem for which competitive fundraising was the solution. The standard neoliberal solution to societal need was to operate more like players in a financial market: stay invested, diversify portfolios, cultivate long-term assets, and maintain ratings. In fact, Canadian charitable donations did drop by almost $1 billion in 2008 and did not recover to 2007 levels until 2014 (Lasby & Barr, 2018; Waldie, 2011). To hear fundraisers speaking at the time, it was as though this drop resulted from their lack of initiative, illustrating how neoliberal entrepreneurialism was internalized and individualized. Even as the financial economy tanked, fundraisers held themselves responsible for meeting targets, almost side-stepping major market collapse as an explanation for the impossibility of their plans.

I have chosen to study fundraisers because of their intermediary positioning between economic elites and institutions that provide social benefit. This book is far from being an exposé of fundraisers' wrong-doing or wrong-thinking, but a study of how they were situated within, navigated, and furthered neoliberal change. Before completing this book, I turned my critical gaze to my own field of post-secondary teaching. Analysing the relationship of neoliberalism to the undergraduate curricular changes that I had been spearheading at Brock University revealed how I, too, work inside of neoliberalism as a university professor and inspired my moving in the direction of radical pedagogy (Raddon & Harrison, 2015).

In this book, I tell the story of how the first generation of fundraising directors and consultants rode the wave of nonprofit expansion. They were positioned to notice that their fundraising could not compensate for tax-funded social provisions that governments had dismantled, but as a group, their career interests and work roles required them to strive to fill the gap. They adhered to neoliberal common sense about the necessity and virtue of their role and their profession's strategic goals.

I found fundraisers' political consensus remarkable considering the diversity of individuals I met: 50 people with varied political identities, career histories, educational backgrounds, and nonprofit sector concerns, from preventing HIV/AIDS to building opera houses. Nonetheless, fundraisers largely shared a set of neoliberal positions and dispositions, as I will describe in each chapter: on the need for less government, lower taxes, and private solutions to social problems; on the merit of entrepreneurialism and letting markets work; on the aim to emulate their seemingly more advanced American counterparts; and on the co-existence of optimism (individual giving can better the world) with fatalism (there is no alternative), along with the disavowal of traditional agonistic politics.

It was a pleasure to meet this talented and indefatigable group. I found them charming, outgoing, intelligent, and enthusiastic for their work. They also modelled the generosity they requested of others. I am grateful for their time and contributions to this research.

St. Catharines, ON, Canada — Mary-Beth Raddon

References

Lasby, D., & Barr, C. (2018). *Thirty Years of Giving in Canada. The Giving Behaviour of Canadians: Who Gives, How, and Why?* https://imaginecanada.ca/sites/default/files/2019-05/30years_report_en.pdf

McGoey, L. (2015). *No Such Thing as a Free Gift: The Gates Foundation and the Price of Philanthropy*. Verso.

Raddon, M.-B., & Harrison, B. (2015). Is Service-Learning the Kind Face of the Neoliberal University? *Canadian Journal of Higher Education, 45*(2), 134–153.

Waldie, P. (2011, October 28). For Canada's Charities, This Is a Time of Crisis and a Moment of Opportunity. *Globe & Mail*. https://www.theglobeandmail.com/life/giving/for-canadas-charities-this-is-a-time-of-crisis-and-a-moment-of-opportunity/article559719/

Acknowledgements

Fifty fundraisers took the time for an in-depth interview with me. I remember these conversations as though they happened yesterday. Thank you for the insight into your day-to-day work and the changes you observed. I marvel at the wide range of your skills, your professional ethics, and your commitment to this work.

I would like to name and thank a few of the people who supported me as I wrote this book. Meaghan Hiller provided valuable research assistance with coding of interviews. Harriet Friedmann affirmed and inspired my slow scholarship. Barb Bloemhof was a wonderful writing companion who celebrated each pomodoro with me. Rebecca Raby followed my ups and downs as an empathic friend and outstanding colleague. Susan Kocen helped me explore interesting layers and levels of many aspects of this project. Susan Petrina gave me invaluable editorial assistance and advice. Bob Hillier was present throughout the research and writing of the manuscript, bringing good conversation, laughter, and a sense of wonder to all my days. Thank you, all.

About the Book

This book contributes to research on the ascendance of neoliberalism in Canada through the vantage point of professional fundraising in the 1990s and 2000s. Fifty high-ranking fundraisers from across Canada were interviewed through 2008 and 2009 about changes they had witnessed since starting their careers. Fundraising as an expert occupation was burgeoning in this period in response to the devolution of state responsibility across the major domains of nonprofit activity: education, health care, social services, the arts, recreation, overseas humanitarian activities, and environmental protection. Welfare state retrenchment left the nonprofit and voluntary sector competing for private sources of funding. The professional fundraisers hired by charities and nonprofits set their sights on the growing fortunes of Canada's highest wealth strata. As these top fundraisers worked to instil a culture of philanthropy, while targeting the ultra-rich, they became both products and promoters of the neoliberal political and cultural reconstruction of Canadian society.

Contents

About the Author

Mary-Beth Raddon is an associate professor and chair of the Department of Sociology at Brock University, St. Catharines, Ontario (Niagara Region), Canada. An economic sociologist, Raddon is interested in how power works in social arrangements in which gifts are monetized or money is gifted. She has researched institutions and practices of inheritance, philanthropy, and local currencies. Raddon is the author of *Community and Money: Men and Women Making Change* (2003), which examined the gendered patterns of reciprocity, work, and shopping that arose as stumbling blocks for people attempting to create community-based currencies and exchange networks to challenge the dominant economy. Raddon teaches qualitative research methods and courses on community engagement at Brock University where she held the Chancellor's Chair for Teaching Excellence (2011–2013). She served as the university's first Faculty Associate for Service Learning (2012–2013) and first faculty chair of the President's Advisory Committee on Human Rights, Equity and Decolonization (2018). She is a former graduate programme director of the MA in Social Justice and Equity Studies and a member of the Social Justice Research Institute at Brock University.

CHAPTER 1

Introduction: Fundraising and Neoliberalization in Canada

Abstract In this chapter, I introduce the idea that professional fundraising is, in the words of one Canadian fundraiser, a "business of hope." I argue that successful fundraising careers provide a lens for understanding Canada's neoliberalization. However, to avoid reducing neoliberalism to a broad abstraction, I make three commitments in this book: first, to show the meaning of neoliberalism through fundraisers' perspectives and through the policy context of their careers in the late 1990s and early 2000s; second, to contrast neoliberalism with the shape of the welfare state that came before; and third, to take a dual political-economic and cultural theoretical approach, holding neoliberalism to be both economic doctrine and governing rationality, revealing neoliberal change to be both structural and cultural.

Keywords Major gifts fundraising • Neoliberalism • Governing rationality • Subjectivity • Positionality

As an undergraduate student, Todd earned money towards his tuition by taking a part-time telefundraising job for his university. On his first shift, he raised over $1000, more than any other student in the call room. He received a $1 bonus, a bag of chips, and something he did not quite grasp at the time: a new career direction. Soon promoted to student supervisor,

M.-B. Raddon, *The Business of Hope*, Palgrave Studies in Third Sector Research, https://doi.org/10.1007/978-3-031-18837-4_1

he worked at the front desk of the Advancement office. From that position, he began to see beyond the telephones. As he recalled:

> I saw the job postings for Advancement Professionals, and I'd see some of them coming to the office dressed up very nicely and so on, in suits like I'm wearing today. And I was like, wow, these guys look like they're doing well. And I saw the pay scale. And it was like, wow, these guys are actually doing well! (Todd)

Upon graduating, Todd jettisoned plans for law school. It was 1995. His university had embarked on a capital campaign, and he had been "tapped on the shoulder" and offered a full-time job doing "grunt work" for donor recognition and special events. He explained, "It was frequent with confident students that if they wanted a job in Alumni Affairs or in Advancement that [the university] would create a place for [recent graduates]." At an event for donors, Todd encountered the university's Vice-President, Advancement for the first time:

> He gave this amazing speech, and these donors are crying and they're so compelled ... [The university] had taken generations of their family from poverty to affluence, and how appreciative they were and how this was the greatest gift that they could possibly give back and gave them the most amount of satisfaction. (Todd)

Todd was also deeply moved, but for different reasons: "I said, 'Boom, this is exactly what I want to do! And one day I want to be better than this guy.'" From that moment, he said, "I actually really have not turned back."

It did not take Todd long to be promoted to Advancement Officer. Three years later, he was still finding thrills in fundraising for the university when he was headhunted to take a position with one of Canada's most prominent disease-related health charities. He turned to a mentor for advice: "I got this call from [the charity] that wants to hire me and they're almost willing to pay me anything I want to go there, which is flattering, but is this the right career step for me?"

Urged to make the move, he went and led the charity's annual gifts programme, but only for a year. "I said, I think I need something that's going to give me a lot more initiative and goals and contact with donors. And I wanted to be in Major Gifts. I didn't want to be pegged as an Annual Giving guy." Whereas annual gifts are usually gifts of cash, given out of income, and used for a variety of general purposes and day-to-day operations, major gifts are given out of assets and designated to endowments, buildings, or significant special needs. Major gifts are often pledged over three to five years on terms stipulated in legal agreements or in the donor's will, in the case of charitable bequests. Major gifts are valued at several times the amount of a typical annual gift. Although organizations receive considerably fewer major gifts, they constitute, by far, the largest percentage of nonprofit revenues.

The challenge of converting prospects to major donors appealed to Todd. So, when a U.S.-based international humanitarian charity advertised the inaugural position of Director of Development, Todd applied and got the job. He coordinated fundraising in over 35 countries, "met some of the most powerful, influential people in the States," and "got to be the front person in terms of solicitation." Returning to Canada after three years, he then led two successive multimillion-dollar campaigns in the position of Campaign Director for two different arts organizations. In 2008, at the time I interviewed him, he had just stepped into a new position, the top fundraising role for the provincial branch of a major national health charity, his sixth appointment in 13 years.

As an emerging specialist in major gifts fundraising, Todd especially "loved the exhilaration of speaking with and engaging people," and he was proud of what his fundraising had accomplished. Beaming with the satisfaction of his work, he described his profession as the "business of hope."

Taking up Todd's expression, this book examines professional fundraising as a "business of hope." By listening to the reflections of 50 experienced Canadian fundraisers on their careers from at least the mid-1990s through to the global financial crisis of 2008, and by situating their stories and perspectives within social change on national and global scales, I consider the political significance of the "business of hope."

At a minimum, "the business of hope" referred to the promise Todd saw in fundraising to satisfy his career ambitions as he hoped to follow the mounting success of his more senior colleagues who had an early start in a burgeoning field. Fundraisers' occupational mobility and achievement is a minor theme of this book. The major subject, and the overarching circumstance that made possible Todd's advancement, is the consolidation of neoliberalism as the prevailing policy framework of the state, and its ascendance as a governing rationality. I argue that the present-day fundraising industry grew out of the merger of business and hope in the form of a utopian market rationality that has been on the ascent since the early 1980s and had emerged as the dominant governing rationality by 1995.

The Participants in This Study

The research for this book draws on qualitative interviews with prominent fundraisers from many nonprofit sub-sectors and specializations working in several major cities across Canada. Todd was one of the most junior of the 50 people I interviewed, with 13 years of full-time work experience. All but one of the 50 had at least 10 years' experience and only 8 others had slightly less experience than Todd. Half had been fundraisers for over 19 years, while seven had started over 25 years ago. The most senior of the participants, Peter, started working in international development in 1975 when fundraising was part of a multifaceted job portfolio. Peter's first full-time fundraising position with a Canadian charity did not begin until the mid-1980s.

As I detail in the Appendix on research methods, the fundraisers who volunteered to be interviewed included 36 women and 18 men. Twelve worked as nonprofit fundraising consultants whose agencies ranged from full-service firms that frequently led multimillion-dollar campaigns to smaller boutique companies that offered specialized expertise. Nine of the fundraisers worked for hospital foundations, and another six were employed by various health charities. Eight worked for educational institutions, mostly universities. Another eight worked for a social service charity, including two community foundations and a charitable organization that supported start-up business ventures. The remaining seven fundraised for organizations that benefited the arts, the environment, international humanitarian causes, and a religious organization. Collectively, over their careers, this group of 50 had held fundraising positions in 283 organizations, and the consultants had served hundreds more nonprofit clients. On the whole, they were experiencing considerable career success. As an indication of their status, 35 of the 50 held the highest possible rank in large nonprofit organizations or consultancy firms, or they had sole responsibility for all fundraising operations of the smaller organizations in which they were employed.

This set of experienced fundraisers had witnessed, experienced, and led profound changes in the fundraising industry. Most were involved in the leadership of professional associations for fundraising, and many had taught in new fundraising training, certification, and educational programmes. Many held the first fundraising position of its kind in their organizations. As a group, they have made their mark on the charitable organizations for which they have worked and on the nonprofit sector overall.

For example, Gordon's 25-year career with two prominent consulting firms had involved international travel and work in all parts of Canada. For the better part of his career, he orchestrated the fundraising of major gifts for large capital campaigns across the province of Ontario. To illustrate his reach, he told a story about the successful end to a capital campaign for a new satellite campus of a university. At a wine and cheese celebration, one of the top volunteers reflected, "You know, Gord, this campaign was so easy, we probably didn't even need you guys." Laughing at the comment, Gordon told me, "I took it as a compliment, the fact that he wasn't there when we were doing the heavy lifting for the building. This was so easy? I'm glad you think that (laughing)." Typical of the fundraisers in this study, Gordon operated in the background and gave volunteers and donors the credit for securing major gift agreements. Only those close to him knew the impact of his work. As he told me, "I can take my kids, and we can go for a drive and wherever it is, I can go, 'Look. I was involved there, and with that. See that thing over there? I raised money for that.'"

Gordon's career impact and Todd's quick rise in the profession occurred in the context of Canada's neoliberalization, which is the driving interest of this book. Though drawing on interviews with fundraisers, this book is not primarily about philanthropic fundraising per se. Research about fundraising from a practitioner's perspective abounds. Indeed, three members of this study had each already authored a book about how to fundraise, and two others were making regular research contributions to trade periodicals. Within the academic literature of philanthropy, however, relatively little has been written about fundraising as an expert occupation. Philanthropy research is substantially focused on donors' motivations for giving, institutional forms of philanthropy and their history, the potential of philanthropy for positive change, and its tendency for harm (Damon & Verducci, 2006; Mack, 2013; Reich et al., 2016). The scant academic research on fundraising has explored topics such as professionalization (Proper & Caboni, 2014; Warren et al., 2016); characteristics of the fundraising workforce (Lindahl & Conley, 2002); the regulation, management, and ethics of fundraising (Lee, 2003; Phillips, 2012); the public image of fundraisers (McGee & Donoghue, 2009); and comparative analysis of national fundraising regimes (Breeze & Scaife, 2015).

By situating the careers of Canadian fundraisers within the welfare state transformations that occurred in the 1990s and early 2000s, this book contributes to research on fundraising and to the broader literature of philanthropy. Ultimately, however, this is a study of social change as it was lived through an occupational group that was thrown up on the wave of neoliberalization and surfed that wave successfully. Just as waves can reshape a shoreline, neoliberalism wrought a new political landscape that fundraisers grew into. By studying fundraisers' accounts of their careers, I aim to understand the relationship of these careers to neoliberalism, how neoliberalization has shaped fundraisers' political subjectivity, and how fundraisers in turn have had a role in shaping Canada's neoliberalization.

How Do You Solve a Problem Like Neoliberalism?

Examined through the rise of the fundraising industry in the 1990s and early 2000s and the perspectives of those leading fundraisers, the object of my research is the process of neoliberalization in Canada. I understand neoliberalism as a set of economic doctrines that restructured the welfare state, and a cultural matrix that became a governing rationality. However, neoliberalism as a change process is difficult to study. How do you catch a wave and pin it down?

The inception of neoliberalism is said to have been the Walter Lippmann Colloquium in Paris in 1938, an event that drew together 26 European and American intellectuals united in their opposition to collectivism and their intention to reconstruct and revitalize liberalism (Dardot & Laval, 2013). Rejecting the classical liberal doctrine of *laissez-faire*, these first neoliberals called for strong states to take an active role in the economy, but to limit that role to establishing and enforcing private property rights, competitive markets, and free trade. Their early meetings and writings laid out the intellectual and policy foundations for an elite-led project that could challenge nineteenth- and twentieth-century social movements and stop governments from implementing policies for wealth redistribution, labour rights, industrial and financial regulation, economic and social planning, and the expansion of social protections, which had widespread popular support (Dardot & Laval, 2013).

Neoliberal ideas remained on the academic and political margins for about three decades, disseminating gradually through the work of well-endowed think tanks, most notably the Mont Pelerin Society founded in 1947. Eminent academic champions based in prestigious universities in Geneva, London, and Chicago worked to give neoliberalism a footing in international governance institutions in the 1970s, which imposed neoliberal programmes of structural adjustment and export-led development in former colonies. The election of Margaret Thatcher in Britain in 1979,

Ronald Reagan in the U.S. in 1980, and Brian Mulroney in Canada in 1984 marked the ascendance of neoliberalism from fringe political philosophy to dominant political-economic orthodoxy. An assortment of pro-market policies and prescriptions typified neoliberalism in the wealthy industrial countries: decreased social spending, reduced labour costs, increased securitization, commodification of public goods, and the devolution of responsibility for human and environmental wellbeing onto smaller social units including families and individuals. The market-oriented rationales for these measures gained ubiquity and the status of common sense. Their outcomes came to appear as normal, just the way things are.

Whereas neoliberalism's proponents initially coined the term to promote a reconstructed liberalism, the concept has come to be deployed within a vast critical literature on neoliberalism's harmful social impacts, such as extreme wealth inequality, sacrifice zones exploited and abandoned by unregulated industry, national and local governments made subservient to speculative capital movements, lives made precarious and cut off from public goods in the push to privatize. The scholarly critique of neoliberalism has been so expansive that charting and comparing theoretical approaches has itself become a key contribution to the literature (England & Ward, 2016; Larner, 2000; Mudge, 2016). Stephanie Mudge (2016), for example, presents three lenses for observing neoliberalism: as an historic phase of capitalism featuring post-Cold War American geopolitical hegemony and the dominance of international financial capital; as a political strategy of governments to reconfigure social life according to a market model; and as a cultural project to instil market values, such as entrepreneurship, competitiveness, and individualism, into daily life. Neoliberalism, she argues, is "irreducibly all of these things" (p. 93).

In view of expanding conceptualizations of neoliberalism, several thinkers problematize the concept (Eagleton-Pierce, 2016; Hall, 2011; Guthman, 2008a; Mudge, 2016; Peck, 2013; Springer, 2016). They worry that neoliberalism's proliferating usage has reduced it to a general-purpose label for changes in contemporary capitalism (Eagleton-Pierce, 2016). In considering whether neoliberalism has turned into a mere buzzword, they have weighed the importance of what the term might still accomplish with the inadequacy of alternatives and concluded that the concept is "fuzzy and politicized, but as-yet *irreplaceable*" (Mudge, 2016, p. 93). However, this questioning of neoliberalism's ontological status—how in seeming to describe everything, it may explain nothing—does not tempt these thinkers to pin down a definition. On the contrary, their concern about the vagueness of "neoliberalism" is matched by their determination not to essentialize a process that has never been singular or stable. They accomplish a non-essentializing analysis through three commitments that guide my own analysis in this book: contextualization, comparison, and broad theorizing.

The first commitment is to study neoliberalism in context and to recognize it as complexly variegated and contradictory. Some scholars have contributed to this stance by writing about local "neoliberalisms" and about "neoliberalization" as an ongoing, adaptive process, not a universal or static condition (Springer, 2016). Others have periodized neoliberalism to emphasize different phases, such as the "roll back" moments of gutting state capacity for social protections, and the "roll out" moments of imposing neoliberal institutional forms (Peck & Tickell, 2002).

To contextualize neoliberalism is to aim for nuanced accounts that connect local to trans-local scales and that observe the dialectical and constitutive relationships between neoliberalisms at different levels of abstraction. Accordingly, this study places neoliberalism in the context of English-speaking Canada during the apogee of neoliberalization, from the mid-1990s to the financial crisis and recession of 2008. By tracing the neoliberal careers and political subjectivities of fundraisers, I describe the workings of particular neoliberal policies and discourses within what Canadian fundraisers call "the sector," the world of nonprofit and voluntary sector institutions they inhabit in their professional lives.

My second commitment follows from the first: to study neoliberalism in relation to its "others." Abstract neoliberalism appears monolithic, but as Peck (2013) argues, "residues of preexisting social formations will never be entirely erased or rendered inert" (p. 154). Vrasti and Montsion (2014, p. 4) remind us to situate neoliberalism as, "the latest phase of a longue durée of capitalist accumulation that goes back to feudal land enclosures, the inquisition, 18th century industrialization and urbanization, 19th century institutions of liberal democracy, and 500 years of colonial and imperial subjugation." Studying neoliberalism in relation to its "others" means viewing it as a process of continuity and change and recognizing ways in which all historic periods of capitalism remain embedded in the present.

Just as neoliberalism is contingent on what came before, neoliberalization is also reactive to its challengers, however distant or marginalized. These challengers include neoliberalism's own variants elsewhere and over time, its crises and disruptions, and "its various competitors, would-be successors, and alternatives" (Peck, 2013, p. 135). For the purpose of this study, the primary challenger to neoliberalization in turn-of-the-century Canada was the residues of post-war Keynesian welfarism, as I will describe in Chaps. 2 and 3. Since the project of free-market reform can never be fully realized, the course of neoliberalism is indeterminate. Identifying neoliberalism's "others" is key to understanding how it achieves its dominance, as well as to imagining possible post-neoliberal political futures.

A third commitment of my analysis of neoliberalism is to bring into dialogue two divergent theoretical approaches—political economy and neo-Foucauldian perspectives—by recognizing their significant overlap without minimizing their disagreement (Guthman, 2008a; Springer, 2012). The political economy literature tends to conceive neoliberalism as an agenda of pro-business activists to redistribute wealth upwards and to fashion the ideological schemas and rhetorical devices, such as appeals to "freedom" and the Thatcherite slogan, "there is no alternative," which make the growth of inequality acceptable (Harvey, 2005, pp. 39–40). The emphasis on neoliberalism's agents and its ideological underpinnings goes a long way to explaining why neoliberalism is not the exclusive domain of the traditional political right. However, political economy approaches struggle to explain the conundrum that even people who reject neoliberalism "writ large" often engage in practices that end up furthering neoliberal culture (Guthman, 2008a, p. 1172), as interviews with nonprofit fundraisers will show. Even fundraisers for agencies whose causes are most compromised by neoliberal programmes (such as those that serve low-income and vulnerable people) appear constrained to speaking within neoliberal categories.

To interpret fundraisers' positionality I engage with scholars inspired by Michel Foucault's approach to power. I especially draw on Wendy Brown (2015), who demonstrates the relevance of Foucault's College de France lectures, *The Birth of Biopolitics, 1978–79*, to understanding how neoliberalism has hollowed out twenty-first-century Western democracy. Following Foucault, Brown argues that one of the most successful neoliberal political strategies has been to demote government while governing populations "at a distance" from coercive state institutions. To do so, neoliberalism constructs society as a self-regulating market, models social relations on competing enterprises, and shapes human subjects as essentially economic creatures: *homo oeconomicus*. In this way, neoliberalism achieves a level of consensus and ubiquity more fundamental than ideology. It governs by managing, "to extend the rationality of the market, the schemes of analysis it proposes, and the decision-making criteria it suggests to areas that are not exclusively or not primarily economic" (Foucault, 2003, p. 207). It governs by inviting its subjects to become self-governing and self-responsible in all areas of life. For example, we see this governance at work in nonprofit management where organizations hold themselves accountable for providing value to stakeholders (including government funders) through annual reporting, audited financials, operational efficiencies, labour flexibility, cost-cutting, and other corporate best practices.

Neoliberal rationality, Brown (2015) argues, inculcates a market orientation as everyday common sense. Governed by this economic rationality, we seek to be self-reliant individuals, engaged in competitive, entrepreneurial activity to enhance our own "human capital." Mirroring the financial economy, our preoccupation is to think of ourselves (as well as our community, workplace, school, or nation) as an enterprise in which we are invested. The language of markets pervades even non-market spheres such as health, relationships, political, and religious life, where we seek to improve our rankings, ratings, and portfolio assets to maximize future value (p. 36).

With Brown (2015) and other neo-Foucauldian scholars, I am interested in how neoliberal economic rationality primes some patterns of thought and being, and obscure others (Guthman, 2008a, 2008b). Specifically, I observe how fundraisers' optimism and idealism are tied to their acceptance of competition, individualism (e.g., as evident in tax-aversion), and sense of the inevitability of public sector restructuring. I also explore how neoliberal discourses substitute market values for the political values associated with the welfare era, and how this substitution makes it possible to rationalize wealth inequality, depoliticize public subsidies of philanthropy, and represent elite activity as democratic, as many fundraisers do.

I will examine these arguments by drawing on fundraisers' interviews in the chapters to come. In Chap. 2, I describe fundraisers' political context with an overview of three areas of policy change that took place simultaneously around the pivotal year 1995 (which happened to be the year that Todd, from the opening of this chapter, began his career): first, the start of downloading, core funding cuts, and the turn to competitive proposal funding of nonprofit social services and the arts; second, the inauguration of the Voluntary Sector Roundtable; and third, changes to the charitable tax credit to incentivize major donations. This constellation of policies laid the groundwork for the two most significant trends in philanthropy that fundraisers identified: more competition among charities and a shift from mass-appeal to major gifts fundraising, resulting in more revenues being generated from fewer donors. Chapter 2 concludes with an overview of a fundamental debate over changing the Income Tax Act to favour major donors.

In the subsequent three chapters, I explore changes in how Canadian fundraisers constructed the meanings of philanthropy, fundraising, and their own careers. In Chap. 3, I describe the shifting emphasis from fundraising for special causes and innovation within an overarching social safety net to the urgency fundraisers felt to create a culture of philanthropy in the face of government retreat from social, cultural, and environmental responsibilities. In Chap. 4, I consider fundraisers' work as a vocation. While most fundraisers would say their purpose was to match donors' philanthropic ambitions with organizations' greatest needs, the field increasingly emphasized donor-centric approaches that placed donors' agency and gratification as fundraisers' priority. I present the story of one fundraiser whose critique of the profession put the dominant practices in vivid relief. In Chap. 5, I look at Canadian fundraisers' tendency to make cross-national comparisons about fundraising landscapes, looking especially to the United States. As neoliberalism erased Canada's social advantage vis-à-vis the U.S. in terms of the generosity of social programmes, fundraisers took up concerns about Canada's "generosity gap" in terms of individual donations. I conclude the book in Chap. 6 by reflecting on fundraisers' contributions to neoliberal politics of hope. The Appendix offers a detailed account of my approach to this research and analysis.

References

Breeze, B., & Scaife, W. (2015). Encouraging Generosity: The Practice and Organization of Fund-Raising across Nations. In P. Wieping & F. Handy (Eds.), *The Palgrave Handbook of Global Philanthropy* (pp. 570–596). Palgrave Macmillan.

Brown, W. (2015). *Undoing the Demos: Neoliberalism's Stealth Revolution*. Zone Books.

Damon, W., & Verducci, S. (Eds.). (2006). *Taking Philanthropy Seriously: Beyond Noble Intentions to Responsible Giving*. Indiana University Press.

Dardot, P., & Laval, C. (2013). *The New Way of the World: On Neoliberal Society* (G. Elliott, Trans.). Verso.

Eagleton-Pierce, M. (2016). *Neoliberalism: The Key Concepts.* Routledge.
England, K., & Ward, K. (2016). Theorizing Neoliberalism. In S. Springer, K. Birch, & J. MacLeavy (Eds.), *The Handbook of Neoliberalism* (pp. 50–60). Routledge.
Foucault, M. (2003). The Birth of Biopolitics. In P. Rabinow & N. Rose (Eds.), *The Essential Foucault: Selections from Essential Works of Foucault, 1954–1984* (pp. 202–207). The New Press.
Guthman, J. (2008a). Neoliberalism and the Making of Food Politics in California. *Geoforum, 39,* 1171–1183.
Guthman, J. (2008b). Thinking Outside the Neoliberal Box: The Micro-politics of Agro-food Philanthropy. *Geoforum, 39,* 1241–1253.
Hall, S. (2011). The Neo-liberal Revolution. *Cultural Studies, 25*(6), 705–728.
Harvey, D. (2005). *A Brief History of Neoliberalism.* Oxford University Press.
Larner, W. (2000). Neo-liberalism: Policy, Ideology, Governmentality. *Studies in Political Economy, 63,* 5–25.
Lee, S. (2003). The regulation of fundraising: in search of the 'public good' or an intractable problem of vested interest? *International Journal of Nonprofit and Voluntary Sector Marketing, 8*(4), 307–314. https://doi.org/10.1002/nvsm.221
Lindahl, W. E., & Conley, A. T. (2002). Literature Review: Philanthropic Fundraising. *Nonprofit Management and Leadership, 13*(1), 91–112. https://doi.org/10.1002/nml.13108
Mack, A. (Ed.). (2013). *Giving: Caring for the Needs of Strangers (Vol. 80).* The New School.
McGee, S., & Donoghue, F. (2009). The Conundrum of Fundraising in Nonprofit Organizations: A Story from Ireland. *Journal of Nonprofit & Public Sector Marketing, 21*(4), 367–383. https://doi.org/10.1080/10495140802662564
Mudge, S. L. (2016). Neoliberalism, Accomplished and Ongoing. In S. Springer, K. Birch, & J. MacLeay (Eds.), *The Handbook of Neoliberalism* (pp. 93–104). Routledge.
Peck, J. (2013). Explaining (with) Neoliberalism. *Territory, Politics, Governance, 1*(2), 132–157.
Peck, J., & Tickell, A. (2002). Neoliberalizing Space. *Antipode, 34*(3), 380–404. https://doi.org/10.1111/1467-8330.00247
Phillips, S. (2012). Canadian Leapfrog: From Regulating Charitable Fundraising to Co-regulating Good Governance. *Voluntas: International Journal of Voluntary and Nonprofit Organizations, 23,* 808–829.
Proper, E., & Caboni, T. C. (2014). Research on Fundraising. In *Institutional Advancement: What We Know* (pp. 25–32). Palgrave Macmillan US.
Reich, R., Cordelli, C., & Bernholz, L. (Eds.). (2016). *Philanthropy in Democratic Societies: History, Institutions, Values.* University of Chicago Press.

Springer, S. (2012). Neoliberalism as Discourse: Between Foucauldian Political Economy and Marxian Poststructuralism. *Critical Discourse Studies, 9*(2), 133–147.

Springer, S. (2016). *The Discourse of Neoliberalism: An Anatomy of a Powerful Idea*. Rowman and Littlefield International.

Vrasti, W., & Montsion, J. M. (2014). No Good Deed Goes Unrewarded: The Values/Virtues of Transnational Volunteerism in Neoliberal Capital. *Global Society, 28*(3), 336–355.

Warren, A., Hoyler, M., & Bell, M. (2016). From 'Shadowy Cabal' to New Profession: Networks of Cooperation and Competition in UK Higher Education Fundraising. *Environment and Planning C: Government and Policy, 34*, 837–854. https://doi.org/10.1177/0263774X15614681

CHAPTER 2

The Neoliberal Foundations of Fundraising, 1995–2008

Abstract This chapter identifies the policy changes, trends, and debates in the years 1995–2008 pivotal to understanding the neoliberal foundations of fundraising in Canada. Neoliberal policy restructured the relationship of government to the nonprofit and voluntary sector by making government funding scarce and conditional on winning short-term contracts. New representatives of the sector did not contest these changes but sought consensus-oriented partnerships with government. Resulting trends included intense competition between nonprofit organizations and growth in the size and number of major gifts, but fewer charitable donations from ordinary Canadians. To keep major gifts flowing and growing, fundraising bodies lobbied successfully for augmented income tax incentives for charitable donations primarily benefitting the wealthiest donors.

Keywords Nonprofit sector restructuring • Contract culture • Shadow state • Voluntary Sector Initiative • Charitable donation tax incentives

Canada's neoliberalization did not start in 1995, but that year was a triple landmark in its history. The year marked a radicalization and intensification of neoliberal fiscal policies to balance government budgets and reduce debt by cutting social spending. The year was also a formative moment for the Canadian nonprofit and voluntary sector when

M.-B. Raddon, *The Business of Hope*, Palgrave Studies in Third Sector Research, https://doi.org/10.1007/978-3-031-18837-4_2

prominent nonprofit directors initiated the Voluntary Sector Roundtable. The year 1995 also signified a watershed for the fundraising profession with an announcement of the first in what would be a series of changes to the tax code for charitable donations. The tax incentives multiplied the number and size of major gifts to Canadian charitable organizations. These three areas of policy change established the demand for fundraisers, gave new status to this occupational group, particularly in large organizations, and gave rise to philanthropic pledges in the hundreds of thousands, millions, and even tens of millions of dollars from Canada's millionaires and billionaires.

Downloading, Core Funding Cuts, and Contract Culture

The first strongly neoliberal Canadian federal government was the Conservative government of Prime Minister Brian Mulroney, elected in 1984, which implemented a programme of trade liberalization, deregulation, privatization, reduced government spending, and contracting out of social programmes. However, the federal Liberal government of Prime Minister Jean Chretien, elected in 1993, pursued a more aggressive agenda of welfare state retrenchment. In 1995, Liberal Finance Minister Paul Martin announced expenditure cuts to every federal government department totalling $25.3 billion over three years. Included in the federal cuts announced in 1995 was $17 billion slashed from transfers to the provinces and territories. For nonprofit and voluntary sector organizations, the direct impact and ongoing ripple effects of these cuts were dramatic, as Peter Elson (2011) explained: "organizations across the spectrum of social policy, environmental, housing, seniors, sports, and arts organizations saw their core funding reduced, eliminated or replaced with [time-] limited fee-for-service contracts [to deliver programs]" (p. 103).

The federal budget cuts were enfolded in a programme of public sector restructuring through which the Liberal government replaced two provincial transfer programmes, Established Program Funding and the Canada Assistance Plan, with a single block transfer for health, education, and welfare called the Canada Health and Social Transfer (CHST). The CHST granted provinces more flexibility in service delivery by removing federal standards while reducing the amount of funding overall. Provinces were forced to undertake massive cuts to social programmes and to find savings through a combination of outsourcing and downloading services to municipalities.

Also, in 1995, compounding the federal retrenchment, Ontarians elected the government of Premier Mike Harris, whose radically neoliberal "Common Sense Revolution" featured cuts to education and healthcare budgets, public sector layoffs, municipal downloading, new "workfare" programmes, and a 21.6% cut to social assistance. The Harris government's neoliberal programme in Ontario followed the lead of Alberta's premier, Ralph Klein. Elected in 1993, Klein's government slashed the 1994 provincial operating budget by 20%, resulting in thousands of public sector layoffs and drastic programme spending cuts to health care, public and post-secondary education, and social services.

Governments' major cost-cutting strategy with nonprofit organizations already responsible for delivering programmes was to axe funding for core administration and introduce competitive bidding for contracts. From this point, most government funding would be delivered in the form of short-term contracts with tighter regulation and inflexible conditions that could change from year to year (Elson, 2011). Amounts would be insufficient to cover operating expenses. Staff time would need to be devoted to applying for contracts, documenting outcomes, and reporting on various metrics to meet new expectations of accountability. Organizations would often be required to secure sources of matching funds as a condition of government funding. Rachel Laforest (2011) summed up the emerging relationship of government to the nonprofit and voluntary sector this way:

> While the federal government was encouraging the participation of voluntary organizations in policy and service delivery on one hand, it was curtailing funding on the other. Core funding programs were subjected to massive cuts, and contracting became the funding instrument of choice. (p. 98)

Nonprofit organizations, faced with insufficient, insecure government funding and demands that they find additional funding streams, leapt into fundraising activities (Laforest, 2011, p. 38).

Suddenly nonprofits were in competition for scarce and shifting pots of government funding and for private donations. With strained resources, they were also called upon to respond to increased social needs. As Rebecca Warnett (2004) explained, the search for new sources of funding brought about organizational metamorphoses as nonprofits shifted their orientation from "mission" to "market":

> Prior to the 1990s, many charities relied heavily on government contributions, and most did not have to concern themselves with raising operational

> funding. Cutbacks changed all this when the government moved to support initiatives that were 'project minded.' Therefore, the sector, once motivated by a sense of mission, is now market driven by a financial need to do well. (pp. 37–8)

The fiscal crisis of the 1990s drove governments to seek to reduce budget deficits and provided the rationale for the new regime of competitive contract funding.[1] Significantly, as Peter Elson (2011) underscores, the contract culture of the nonprofit sector was not reversed in subsequent periods of economic growth and fiscal surplus, and the changed character of the nonprofit sector starting in 1995 took on permanence (p. 89).

The Voluntary Sector Roundtable

Attempts to define the nonprofit and voluntary sector, often shortened to "the sector," are complicated by the wide range of forms nonprofit organizations take. Common associations, such as being dependent on voluntarism and donations or providing charitable services, are neither universal to all nonprofit organizations nor exclusive to nonprofits alone (Hall, 1992). Definitions that position the nonprofit sector as intermediate to the state and market are also confounded by the hybridity of some organizations that share features with business or government (Frumkin, 2016). What nonprofit organizations do share, according to Hall (1992), is "their concrete historical association with a particular institutional culture, a configuration of values, resources, organizational technologies, legal infrastructure, and styles of leadership." This institutional culture emerged in the course of political struggle, "struggle over the power of the institutions that set the public's moral and perceptual agendas" (Hall, 1992, p. 2). The year 1995 turned out to be pivotal in terms of the way that political leadership came to be organized, which would shape and define the institutional culture of the Canadian nonprofit sector henceforth.

The Canadian state and nonprofit and voluntary sector organizations have always had an interdependent relationship involving substantial state funding, regulation, and political collaboration (Valverde, 1995). However, until the 1990s, the nonprofit sector lacked a strong collective identity, a national umbrella body, and representational leadership that could coordinate political responses and advocate on behalf of the sector. According to Laforest (2011), prior to the mid-1990s, "voluntary organizations did not even recognize themselves as belonging to a larger community called the 'voluntary sector'" (p. 29). Heads of the major charities communicated with governments individually about the concerns of their own organizations. In 1995, in response to the federal government's programme review and announced budget cuts, the leaders of 12 national nonprofit organizations convened the Voluntary Sector Roundtable (VSR) to set a common agenda. Laforest (2011) called this gathering a turning point because it was the first time that organizational leaders identified themselves as representing shared interests belonging to what they chose to call the "voluntary sector" (p. 51). The VSR legitimized the nonprofit and voluntary sector as a political constituency, not an aggregation of organizations (Laforest, 2011, p. 3).

The Voluntary Sector Roundtable was an informal, open coalition that came together to discuss strategic responses, common interests, and ways to provide a voice for the nonprofit and voluntary sector in legislative and regulatory decisions of government. The VSR set the stage for the Voluntary Sector Initiative (VSI), launched by the federal government in 2000. Given a budget of $95 million over five years, the VSI attempted to bring civil servants into conversation with sector representatives about the roles and relationship of government and nonprofit and voluntary organizations in Canada's welfare state. With the election of the Conservative government of Stephen Harper in 2006, the VSI was discontinued and another round of deep cuts ensued, especially to the arts and culture sector. By this point, however, the political work to position the nonprofit and voluntary sector as a partner with government had been accomplished.

To return to Hall's (1992) argument that the nonprofit sector is defined by an institutional culture that emerges in political struggle, the formation of the VSR was a defining moment. As Laforest (2011) notes, participation in the VSR was open to nonprofit leaders, but it was the heads of "large, well-established, mainstream national voluntary and charitable organizations" who dominated the agenda (p. 54). These leaders eschewed oppositional politics in favour of what they saw as "tremendous opportunities to transform their political standing by shifting their language to focus on partnership and collaboration" (p. 54). Their priority in the short and intermediate term was not advocacy for restored core funding or against the emerging contract regime. Rather, "a strategic decision was made from the start not to act confrontationally, but to portray the sector as a responsible partner capable of engaging Canadians" (Laforest, 2011,

p. 55). The significance of the VSR, then, was its role in renegotiating a relationship of the state and nonprofit sector on neoliberal terms, which is to say, in a depoliticized way, accommodating to public sector restructuring and retrenchment, and giving primacy to reputational issues.

Tax Incentives for Philanthropy

Along with the cuts to core funding, the 1995 federal budget announced the first in what would become a series of amendments to Canada's Income Tax Act to expand incentives for philanthropy. These changes in charitable tax policy signalled the government's expectation that nonprofit organizations would mitigate the impact of cutbacks through fundraising. Commenting on the 1996 Budget Plan, Elson (2011) noted, "The message was clear: from now on the voluntary sector would have to rely on the market and donors, not government, for financial support" (p. 106). Of the more than 20 new charitable donations tax incentives the Department of Finance introduced between 1996 and 2009, two types of changes have defined Canada's tax policy on charitable giving and have set a course for nonprofit and voluntary sector fundraising (Burrows, 2009, p. 4).

The first change of major significance that came into effect in 1996 applied to the annual limit on donations that qualify for the charitable income tax credit. The federal tax credit for charitable donations above $200 was based on the top marginal tax rate no matter the tax filer's income, but a ceiling was placed on how much may be claimed for the credit.[2] In 1996, the limit on allowable donations was raised from 20 to 50% of the donor's net income. In 1997, this contribution limit was raised again, this time to 75% of net income or 100% of net income for the year of, or preceding, the taxpayer's death.

The second way the federal government began to change the tax code was to encourage donations of certain appreciated assets, specifically, publicly traded securities (shares, bonds, stock options, mutual fund units), culturally significant properties, and ecologically sensitive land. Prior to 1997, when publicly traded securities (and other eligible assets) were donated to a registered charity the capital gains tax was applied.[3] This meant, for the purpose of tax calculations, the donor was deemed to have sold that donated asset for its fair market value. As the inclusion rate at the time was 75%, the donor was required to add 75% of the realized value of the asset to their taxable income, and to pay tax on that amount at their marginal income tax rate.

In 1997, the capital gains tax on charitable donations of publicly traded securities was temporarily halved. This measure was made permanent in 2001. In 2000, the Liberal government under Jean Chretien reduced Canada's inclusion rate for taxing capital gains from 75 to 67%, and later the same year dropped the rate to 50%. When applied to charitable donations, this lowered federal rate meant that donors of publicly traded securities were required to declare as taxable income only half of 50%, or 25%, of the realized value of their donated asset. These donors of capital assets were always also able to claim the charitable tax credit calculated on the full value of the donation. For such donations, the charitable tax credit more than offset the capital gains tax.

In 2006, Stephen Harper's Conservative government followed a pattern set by the Liberals shortly following the 1995 cuts. The 2006 federal budget cut $1 billion of funding to the nonprofit sector. In conjunction with this cut, the government announced another expansion of the charitable tax credit. This time the capital gains tax was completely eliminated on gifts of appreciated publicly traded securities and selected other types of capital property (Elson, 2011, p. 109).

Together these changes have made Canada's tax policy the most favourable of any industrialized countries towards individuals who wish to offset income taxes through charitable gifts, especially those able to donate financial assets (Burrows, 2009, p. 4; Standing Committee on Finance, 2013, p. 9). For cash gifts above a threshold of $200, donors received a charitable tax credit of between 40 and 57% of the value of the gift, depending on province (as provincial and federal credits are combined). The tax credit for gifts of publicly traded securities typically amounted to 60 to 67% of the value of the donation taking into consideration the avoidance of capital gains tax (Standing Committee on Finance, 2013).

Beyond generosity to individual donors, Canada's incentive system was "unique in the world," according to Malcolm Burrows (2009, p. 6), because of how the charitable tax credit embedded social policy. The changed rules were exclusively oriented towards high-income Canadians, those with the prospect of making large gifts relative to their incomes, as well as those who could donate capital assets. Ordinary donors making average gifts were not able to benefit in any way from the overhauled rules. More significantly, the degree to which the new rules offset income taxes of high-income donors indicated a shift in the philosophy of how social priorities would be funded, as Burrows (2009) explained:

> The increased contribution limits implicitly signaled that charitable giving is no longer a supplementary public benefit activity of lesser importance than direct government programs [funded by taxes]. … For the first time, registered charities are considered to be as valid and as important a deliverer of public benefits as government. (p. 6)

These new incentives for exceptional gifts had their intended effect of stimulating elite philanthropy. In the decade prior to 1995, the inflation-adjusted value of tax-receipted donations reported to Revenue Canada was relatively steady until 1996 when it jumped by 11.7% over the 1995 level (Duff, 2001, p. 423). In the years that followed, the new tax incentives were responsible for "prompting unprecedented large gifts and increasing overall giving by 140%, from $3.6 billion in 1995 to $8.65 billion in 2007" (Burrows, 2009, p. 5). From 1997 to the time of the financial crisis of 2008 the value of donated shares alone was approximately $3 billion (Burrows, 2009, p. 11).

To summarize, three policy developments all occurred around 1995 and combined to create a growing demand for fundraisers. First, government cuts to core funding of nonprofit organizations produced a sector expected to compete for contracts, diversify revenues, and deliver more with less. Second, the Voluntary Sector Roundtable came to represent a sector seeking political respectability and partnership rather than contestation on behalf of struggling subsectors. Third, new charitable tax incentives were introduced to encourage more wealthy Canadians to make major philanthropic gifts, especially consisting of publicly traded securities.

Interviewed in 2008, Heather, a hospital foundation president with 19 years' experience, told me, "Every organization under the sun is fundraising—every social service organization that used to have sufficient funding." Similarly, Lynn, the director of a health charity with 14 years' experience, explained, "There's more organizations that want to fundraise, and there's more people coming into fundraising, but there's still not enough [fundraisers], and there's not enough people with experience."

The remainder of this chapter extends this overview of the neoliberal context of fundraising in Canada in 1995 through 2008 by examining the most significant changes fundraisers have witnessed over their careers by their own accounts. The two trends that the fundraisers in this study commonly identified were, first, the increased competition among charities, not just for donors but also for experienced fundraising staff, and second, the growth in the magnitude and frequency of major gifts along with the declining number of "ordinary" donors. Exploring these trends will set the stage for subsequent chapters by identifying fundraising as both a growth industry in a neoliberal policy era and an expert occupation enmeshed in neoliberal rationality.

Fundraising Trends: "Competition for the Donor Dollar"

Early in the interviews, I asked fundraisers to identify the most significant changes in the fundraising landscape they had witnessed during their career. A seasoned executive with an international fundraising consultancy, Samantha, summed up one of the two most common sets of responses:

> The most important change? I would say the competitiveness is like it's never been before. There's so much competition for the donor dollar. (Samantha)

And Ruby, a veteran fundraiser of 20 years, who also held a senior leadership position for national consulting firm, elaborated on how the growing competition among charities applied to competition for fundraising personnel as well as donors:

> I think [we are seeing] growth in the number of charities and fund development growing as a business because so many charities who used to get government funding 10 years ago now no longer get it, so they've had to turn to fundraising to offset the financial loss. And so, you've got more charities, more organizations who need more fundraisers because they are no longer getting the government funding they used to have. Put those together. Even though more people are going into fundraising, it's still not enough to meet those two driving factors. (Ruby)

Several participants commented on the demand for fundraisers leading to high rates of turnover. A survey of members of the Association of Fundraising Professionals found that Canadian fundraisers were staying at one job for 3.8 years on average (Healey et al., 2010, p. 13), but the rate of job switching in certain specialties and ranks alarmed the fundraisers I interviewed. Vivian, who had worked at three international nongovernmental organizations over 24 years, argued: "The variety of the causes and the sheer size of the sector has grown tremendously, and with that, the competition for experienced fundraisers has become desperate and dire."

Lynn, cited earlier, called the turnover in the industry "insane," adding: "Every organization is poaching each other … so the people with experience will get poached by one organization or another." A senior executive of a boutique consulting firm, Sherry, underscored the seriousness of the problem by observing that, "the headhunters themselves are worried about what's going on!"

As fundraisers' comments illustrate, this pervasive competition was an outcome of the nonprofit sector restructuring that escalated around 1995. However, many fundraisers also evaluated the changing nonprofit sector through a neoliberal rationality that sees competition as positive. Neoliberal thought constructs an opposition between "unaffordable" government and "efficient" markets, and argues for organizing social life along a market model involving competition (Miller & Rose, 2008, p. 80). Applying the general precept that more competition is a good thing, some fundraisers rationalized the changes that created competition.

Welfare state analysis of this period affirms fundraisers' observations that competition—not fiscal constraint, decentralizing services, or other objectives—was the overwhelming outcome of nonprofit sector restructuring. For example, Jennifer Wolch (1990) famously pointed out that an earlier round of contracting-out services to nonprofit organizations in the United States did not reduce the fiscal or administrative size of the state but grew what she has termed the "shadow state," which she defined as:

> a para-state apparatus comprised of voluntary organizations … administered outside of traditional democratic politics. It is charged with major collective service responsibilities previously shouldered by the public sector. Yet it remains within the purview of state control. (p. 4; see also Mitchell, 2001)

For Evans et al. (2005, p. 1), the nonprofit sector's reconstruction as a para-state apparatus presented a paradox of "centralized decentralization." While decentralizing service delivery did not substantially change the state's welfare functions, it did intensify the relationship of nonprofit organizations to the state. Ultimately, neoliberal restructuring was less about shrinking government or practicing fiscal restraint than enacting a new political logic that "has shifted from entitlement to obligation" (Hartman, 2005, p. 61). In other words, nonprofit organizations and other social entities would be required to prove they deserve to exist by dominating in competitive fields.

Many fundraisers disclosed that competition among nonprofit organizations for regular donors and wealthy prospects, for government contracts, and for experienced staff marked their careers with uncertainty, stress, and burnout. Even so, my study participants generally accepted competition, and some celebrated it. For example, Carolyn, who moved into positions of increased responsibility through her career working for a social service agency, national health charity, children's charity, and university-based medical research institute, interpreted the growth in the number of charitable organizations as a signalling the maturity of "free market philanthropy":

> More charities [means], I don't even think more competition, but more choice. A growth in choice of charities. … It's about choice and competition and that makes us all better. Isn't that how it works? Free market philanthropy! If you're not good, people aren't going to choose you and all the better. You'll disappear. You won't get funds. If you're good, [voice trails off]. That's competition. That's a positive thing. (Carolyn)

More competition among nonprofit and voluntary sector organizations, as Carolyn explained, created quasi-markets for charitable donations and larger philanthropic gifts. Governments continued to financially support nonprofit organizations by granting contracts and subsidizing charitable donations with the tax credit. However, introducing competition fundamentally altered the process of determining which organizations and activities would receive state support. Those decisions would be removed from the traditional political sphere and made to appear as though donors sifted winners from losers in a marketplace of charities.

Fundraising Trends: "Fewer People Giving More Money"

The second significant change fundraisers observed in their careers was the increased size of the largest donations. Five members of this study held the position of Vice President or Director of Major Gifts for their organization. Several others solicited major gifts for capital campaigns or had mixed portfolios that included major gift fundraising. One of the Directors of Major Gifts, Nicole, put it simply: "Every year the major gifts get bigger."

In fact, whatever the fundraisers' current specialization or assignment, the growth of major gift fundraising arose as a topic of every interview because this trend was so relevant to their work and careers. "People have huge expectations for major gifts," explained Vivian, adding that the revenue growth was inflating fundraising targets across the board and creating "immense" pressure on fundraisers.

> We have unrealistic expectations as a sector, so what's happened in the last few years is that all of us have decided to double our income. ... [She quickly names six large charities with the declared goal of doubling fundraised revenue.] We've all decided that doubling is possible because we've all had lots of growth in the last little while, but the donor base on a macro level does not exist. It's not sustainable. (Vivian)

Together with the arrival of huge donations, fundraisers were seeing a parallel trend: declining numbers of regular donors from year to year. The percentage of Canadians who claimed the charitable tax credit steadily declined from approximately 30% of tax filers in the early 1990s to 24% in 2007 and 21% in 2015 (KCI Philanthropy, 2017). Some of this drop may have been the result of spouses starting to combine charitable donation receipts, but another measure of broad-based giving, survey data on self-reported donations from the Canadian Survey of Giving, Volunteering, and Participating, corroborated the downward trend seen in the income tax data (KCI Philanthropy, 2017). Additionally, the number of Canadians who contributed to their own registered retirement savings programme (RRSP) declined at the same rate as charitable giving, which suggests a common cause: creeping financial stress of middle and low-income households (KCI Philanthropy, 2017). Putting the growth in major gifts together with the drop-in overall rates of donating, Sherry attributed both trends to the changing distribution of wealth in Canadian society: "I think we're seeing it [wealth inequality] in terms of fewer people giving more money and we're seeing the big mega gifts coming from that top 10 percent."

The growing concentration of wealth at the top is a pre-condition for major gifts, but the six- to eight-figure donations that began in the mid-1990s would not have happened were it not for the new income tax incentives. To verify the impact of the changed tax rules, David Duff (2001) analysed Revenue Canada data on tax filers in six income classes who claimed the charitable tax credit in the years 1995 and 1996, before and after the contribution limits were raised enabling large gifts to offset income taxes, an incentive that is useful only for high-income tax filers.

Duff's analysis showed that Canadians who earned $100,000–$250,000 increased their share of charitable donations compared to other income groups by almost 1% over the previous year, while tax filers in the top group earning over $250,000 increased their share of donations by almost 3%. As early as 1996, then, "increases in the maximum donations that can be claimed in a taxation year, [had] altered the distribution of charitable donations claimed by income class, significantly increasing the percentage of charitable donations claimed by the highest income groups" (Duff, 2001, p. 423). Accordingly, fundraisers spoke of the changed rules for the tax credit as another significant change in their careers.

In light of this pattern of more fundraised revenue coming from fewer donors, my interview participants explained that the most effective strategy for many organizations was to prioritize major gift solicitation. For example, Jacob, who had worked for two universities and a social services charity over his 19-year career, explained how a "90–10 rule" now guides his efforts:

> You work really, really hard, and you get like $100 on average from 40,000 people, and that's wonderful. That's one program. You could put the same amount of effort in and be getting the same amount of money from 20 people, and there are only so many of those people. (Jacob)

But for Andrew, who entered fundraising in mid-career and had devoted 16 years to directing a large fundraising staff at a single institution, the more-from-fewer trends meant shifting his fundraising strategy to a new extreme:

> When you look at the numbers, it's not the 80–20 rule anymore. It's probably the 95–5 percent rule. In other words, 95% of our money is coming from 5% of the people who give. (Andrew)

Major gifts fundraising approaches were spreading across more types of fundraising organizations, as Joan attested. In her 22-year career, Joan had fundraised for Indigenous and environmental organizations and a hospital foundation before becoming the director of a mid-sized social services charity.

> You have to concentrate on, where is your greater return going to be? So, if you concentrate on five people that are going to give you $5,000, you're going to get $25,000. Or do you spend the same amount of time where there's potential to get a million dollars? (Joan)

Thus, competition to lower fundraising costs per dollar donated drove the emphasis on major gifts fundraising as this approach was the most administratively efficient.

The growth of major gifts was causing fundraisers to rethink the donor pyramid model. The pyramid is a metaphor for the distribution of an organization's supporters according to the size of their gifts. A large number of first-time and occasional donors who give small amounts comprise the base. Donors who give larger amounts and tend to be regular givers make up the next tier, and a select group of generous "angels" appears at the apex. Conventional fundraising thinking had been that fundraisers should work to move people up the pyramid by engaging their interest in the organization, encouraging them to become monthly or annual donors, and then making personal appeals to solicit extraordinary pledges and bequests from the most committed donors. But the emerging wisdom was that the 5% of donors who generate 95% of revenues were unlike donors lower on the pyramid. They might never have been annual givers, their motives might differ, and they might require years of concerted cultivation and negotiation, which was the work of dedicated major gifts staff in large organizations. Consequently, as Jacob observed, "all the big charities are all competing for those people at the top who have the power and the wealth and the influence and, presumably, the desire [to give]."

A Debate About Tax Policy for Philanthropy

This overview of trends in the field of nonprofit fundraising and philanthropy: competition for donor dollars and more-from-fewer points to a fundamental social policy debate centred on the charitable tax credit. Two Canadian tax law experts who have participated publicly in this debate, Jack Mintz and Neil Brooks, represent the opposed positions. Mintz is an economist and professor at the University of Calgary business and law schools. Brooks is a lawyer and emeritus professor at Osgoode Hall Law School, York University. Both point out that the charitable tax incentive is a form of tax expenditure, what Matthew Bishop calls, "a kind of outsourced form of public spending" (Bishop, 2013, p. 488). Tax expenditures lower government revenues to promote favoured activities, in this case, charitable donations. The size of the charitable tax credit varies by province because provincial credits are added to federal credits. It also depends on the donor's income tax bracket and whether the gift is made up of capital assets, but for most major gifts, the donors' charitable tax credit amounts to well over half the value of the gift and as much as two-thirds. For example, a gift of a million dollars would cost the donor less than $500,000, and cost governments more than $500,000 in foregone tax revenue.

In a National Post column, Jack Mintz argued for this government subsidy of philanthropy as a policy to generate competition among charities:

> The combined charitable tax credit and capital gains exemption now make up a substantial share of donation costs [to governments]. If governments are paying most of the costs, a taxpayer might wonder why governments don't just fund charities directly. But it would be unwise to create a system where politics decide which charities get funded. A system where charities compete for our gifts better ensures funds go to the worthiest causes. (Mintz, 2016)

Brooks (2001), writing shortly after the tax incentive for donated securities was enhanced for a third time, presented a retort to this line of argument. He countered that the tax expenditure for large philanthropic donations only appears to sideline politics. Incentivizing philanthropy is fundamentally political in the way it favours the decision-making power and priorities of a small strata of the wealthiest members of society. Brooks wrote:

> This debate over enriching the tax credit for charitable contributions is not about "whether Canadians should be allowed to keep more of their hard-earned income" or about "encouraging altruism." It is about the meaning of citizenship and about concepts of social rights, equality and entitlement. Also, ultimately, it is a debate about who will exercise power in Canadian society. (Brooks, 2001, p. 477)

Most fundraisers in my study who had thought about this debate were on side with Jack Mintz. They also supported their representative bodies, such as the Canadian Association of Fundraising Professionals, in lobbying for stronger tax incentives. For example, Frances, the President of a community foundation who had also fundraised for health care, social services, and post-secondary education during her 25-year career, would advise prospective major donors of their opportunity to exercise power directly through their philanthropy:

> The other thing that I say is you're going to be supporting the sector one way or the other. Either you're going to be doing it through tax or you're going to be doing it through making your own donation. By making your own donation, you can decide which part of the society you want to help. And through tax, you probably have less control over that. So personally, I say give it through philanthropy. (Frances)

Frances illustrated how fundraisers' competitive work to facilitate elite philanthropy contributed to making charitable worthiness a matter for rich people to define. How fundraisers responded to warnings such as Brooks' (2001) about the threats of philanthropy to concepts of citizenship, social rights, equality, and entitlement sheds light on how neoliberalism works as a governing rationality, which I will explore in the chapters that follow.

Notes

1. For analysis of the origins of state fiscal crises and national government responses, I recommend the work of economic sociologist Fred L. Block. Focusing on the United States, Block described how an aggressive programme of government deficit-reduction through social spending cuts eclipsed other viable policy options for addressing the root problem of unregulated flows of capital across national borders (see Block, 1996).
2. After the federal government raised the top marginal income tax rate in 2016, the charitable income tax credit was based on a three-tier assessment. As before, the first $200 of a tax filer's donations received a 15% credit (the first tier). Gifts above $200 received a tax credit valued at 29% of donations exceeding $200 (the second tier). Some donors qualified for a combination of 29% and 33% (the third tier) when their annual income was above $200,000, putting them in the new top tax bracket.
3. The capital gains tax is a tax on the realized value (gains) when an investment asset, such as shares in mutual funds or a rental property, is sold. A certain percentage of those gains, called the "inclusion rate," is added to taxable income. In the mid-1990s, the inclusion rate for capital gains was 75% of the realized value of the sold asset. When the inclusion rate was 75%, for example, this meant the taxpayer who sold a capital asset was taxed on their annual income plus 75% of the capital gain from that sale. The tax rate was the marginal tax rate for the taxpayer's income level. In the year 2000, the capital gain inclusion rate was reduced from 75% to 66.33% and reduced again to 50% that same year.

References

Bishop, M. (2013). Philanthrocapitalism: Solving Public Problems through Private Means. *Social Research: An International Quarterly, 80*(2), 473–490.

Block, F. L. (1996). *The Vampire State and Other Myths and Fallacies about the U.S. Economy.* The New Press.

Brooks, N. (2001). The Tax Credit for Charitable Contributions: Giving Credit Where None Is Due. In J. Phillips, B. Chapman, & D. Stevens (Eds.), *Between State and Market: Essays on Charities Law and Policy in Canada* (pp. 457–481). McGill-Queen's University Press.

Burrows, M. (2009). Charitable Tax Incentives in Canada: Overview and Opportunities for Expansion. *The Philanthropist, 22*(1), 3–23.

Duff, D. G. (2001). Charitable Contributions and the Personal Income Tax: Evaluating the Canadian Credit. In J. Phillips, B. Chapman, & D. Stevens (Eds.), *Between State and Market: Essays on Charities Law and Policy in Canada.* McGill-Queen's University Press.

Elson, P. (2011). *High Ideals and Noble Intentions: Voluntary Sector-Government Relations in Canada.* University of Toronto Press.

Evans, B., Richmond, T., & Shields, J. (2005). Structuring Neoliberal Governance: The Nonprofit Sector, Emerging New Modes of Control and the Marketisation of Service Delivery. *Policy and Society, 24*(1), 73–79.

Frumkin, P. (2016). The Idea of a Nonprofit and Voluntary Sector. In J. Steven Ott & L. A. Dicke (Eds.), *The Nature of the Nonprofit Sector* (pp. 11–21). Westview Press.

Hall, P. D. (1992). *Inventing the Nonprofit Sector and Other Essays on Philanthropy, Voluntarism, and Nonprofit Organizations.* John Hopkins University Press.

Hartman, Y. (2005). In Bed with the Enemy: Some Ideas on the Connections between Neoliberalism and the Welfare State. *Current Sociology, 53*(1), 57–73.

Healey, R., Bartolini, B., Maehara, P. V., & Williams, C. (2010). *2009–2010 AFP Compensation and Benefits Study.* Association of Fundraising Professionals.

Laforest, R. (2011). *Voluntary Sector Organizations and the State: Building New Relations.* UBC Press.

Miller, P., & Rose, N. (2008). *Governing the Present.* Cambridge, UK: Polity Press.

Mintz, J. (2016, April 12). Liberals Are Right to Cancel Charitable Tax Breaks. *Financial Post.* Retrieved from http://business.financialpost.com/fp-comment/jack-mintz-liberals-are-right-to-cancel-charitable-tax-breaks

Mitchell, K. (2001). Transnationalism, Neo-liberalism, and the Rise of the Shadow State. *Economy and Society, 30*(2), 165–198.

KCI Philanthropy. (2017, Spring). Giving by Canadians. *Philanthropic Trends Quarterly.* http://kciphilanthropy.com/download_trends/2017_1/pt-2017-01.pdf

Standing Committee on Finance. (2013). James Rajotte, Chair. *Tax Incentives for Charitable Giving in Canada*. 41st Parliament, 1st Session. http://www.ourcommons.ca/DocumentViewer/en/41-1/FINA/report-15

Valverde, M. (1995). The Mixed Social Economy as a Canadian Tradition. *Studies in Political Economy, 47*(Summer), 33–60.

Warnett, R. (2004). Canadian Fundraising. *New Directions for Philanthropic Fundraising, 2004*(46), 37–52.

Wolch, J. (1990). *The Shadow State: Government and the Voluntary Sector in Transition*. The Foundation Center.

CHAPTER 3

"Do or Die": Creating a Culture of Philanthropy

Abstract This chapter examines fundraisers' aspirations to introduce a "culture of philanthropy," which was a moral and political vision of widespread giving and major philanthropy as vehicles for generosity, democracy, and social transformation. Although fundraisers held a range of political identities from social democratic to conservative, they defined the culture of philanthropy through neoliberal discourses of individualism, personal responsibility, competitiveness, entrepreneurship, devolution of government, and low taxation, and against a welfarist programme of progressive taxation and state-funded services.

Keywords Charitable income tax credit • Welfare state • Philanthrocapitalism • Competition • Tax expenditure

Fundraising was a second career for Mavis. As a wills and estates lawyer, she took notice of press attention to the idea that a generation of seniors had amassed substantial wealth and would ultimately bequeath some of it to charity (Dalby, 2003; Fennell et al., 1990). "This seemed to be a new part of fundraising," she said, "and it was something that really interested me." So, she left her law practice in the mid-1990s to work for a major arts organization, setting up its first formal planned giving programme. After seven years, she joined a large community foundation where she worked

M.-B. Raddon, *The Business of Hope*, Palgrave Studies in Third Sector Research, https://doi.org/10.1007/978-3-031-18837-4_3

to create endowment funds. In this position she discovered that small charities needed legal expertise if they were to start receiving charitable bequests on their own. Within a few years, she had started an independent consulting business to help agencies that lacked specialized fundraising staff to manage planned giving.

Like other fundraisers I interviewed, Mavis provided leadership within more than one professional association for fundraisers and specialists. Beyond the work of advancing the fundraising industry by enhancing its reputation, promoting ethical practices, accrediting members, keeping their knowledge up to date, offering mentorship, and so on, these professional associations adopted a more ambitious political agenda. Mavis summed it up with an expression I heard frequently in my interviews: "You know," she said of her associations' work, "we're creating a *culture of philanthropy*."

This chapter examines the goal of creating a culture of philanthropy as an expression of fundraisers' political agency within the context of Canada's neoliberalization. As I described in Chap. 2, and as Mavis explained further, the imperative to fundraise arose when the nonprofit sector experienced "a pretty dramatic cutback in government funding a decade ago, at least." She elaborated on how, beyond the cuts, nonprofit funding arrangements had been permanently restructured:

> There's now an expectation on the part of government. I mean, they still really do the majority of the funding, particularly for social service groups and that sort of thing, but there is an expectation that I'm finding on the part of the government for the organizations they're funding to be proactive in terms of fundraising in the private sector. (Mavis)

Fundraising grew up out of a welfare state crisis, as Mavis explained:

> If these organizations want to survive and if we don't want to see our social safety net totally obliterated, they've got to go into philanthropy. [...] It's kind of, do or die. (Mavis)

Given the requirement to secure funding from private sources, nonprofit leaders and fundraisers began to recognize that their success required broad-based change—the inception of a culture of philanthropy.

Fundraisers like Mavis, who were aware of how neoliberal policy had "caused tremendous stress in the sector," took up the challenge of growing a philanthropic culture by providing its political rationale. On the one hand, she lamented that the "social safety net" had been lacerated. "On the other hand," she said, "I do see some benefit in terms of having a society where individuals are more active in terms of their community, a sense of being involved and maybe move away from this expectation, well it's the responsibility of somebody else." Lowering citizens' expectations of government, then, and instilling a sense of personal responsibility to help fund the work of nonprofit institutions had become a political mission.

Promoting a Culture of Philanthropy Through Charitable Tax Policy

Rather than take up collective advocacy to restore direct public funding of nonprofit institutions, fundraisers worked through their professional associations to lobby for policies that would engrain philanthropy culturally and institutionally. Their most concerted appeal was for revisions to the Income Tax Act to enrich existing charitable tax incentives in ways designed to stimulate large gifts, such as exempting donors from paying capital gains tax on certain donated capital assets, as explained in Chap. 2.

Successive reports of Senate committees looking into tax treatment of donations reveal the strength of fundraisers' advocacy. In 2004, for example, the Standing Senate Committee on Banking, Trade and Commerce recommended that the government eliminate capital gains tax on donations of publicly traded securities after multiple professional bodies associated with the fundraising industry dominated two days of hearings (Standing Senate Committee, 2004).[1]

In a critique of the prior Department of Finance decision in 2001 to make permanent the 1997 temporary halving of the capital gains tax on donated publicly traded securities and certain other forms of capital property, tax law scholar Lisa Philipps (2003) problematized the Department's reliance on research by nonprofit sector advocacy bodies. "Such advocacy is entirely legitimate," Philipps wrote, "in view of the increasing responsibilities being given to charitable organizations in Canadian society and the accompanying pressure on their resources" (2003, p. 924). However, given the nonprofit sector's stake in generating large philanthropy, she argued, independent analysis was also needed to assess whether this policy instrument, known as a tax expenditure—an attempt to promote a behaviour by reducing an otherwise applicable tax—was both cost-effective and fair.

To prove cost-effective, the nonprofit sector gains from donated securities would need to more than offset the cost to government in foregone taxes. It turned out that more securities were donated after 1997, but the increase in the total value of donations of all forms from 1998 to 2000 was consistent with the pattern of year-to-year increases over the previous 15 years. The prior rule change in 1996, to raise the ceiling on allowable donations, more clearly triggered an increase in aggregate giving than did the reduced capital gains tax on donated securities in 1997. Moreover, the increased donations of publicly traded securities did not necessarily represent new charitable sector revenues. Rather than giving more, many donors may have simply opted for the more tax-advantageous form of giving (Philipps, 2003, p. 921).

Evaluating the fairness of the reduction (and subsequent elimination in 2006) of capital gains taxes on donated securities requires attention to how the charitable income tax credit itself is already weighted in favour of affluent donors by crediting large donations at a higher rate per dollar donated. To be specific, the federal charitable income tax credit is calculated using the lowest federal marginal tax rate (15% as of the year 2000) for donations under $200 and the highest marginal tax rate (29%) for donations above that threshold.[2] Similarly, provinces calculate an additional charitable income tax credit based on the same $200 donation threshold, with the lowest marginal tax rate applied to small donations and the highest rate applied to amounts over $200. This two-tiered structure (three-tiered since 2006), which provides the most tax assistance to those who donate more than $200 annually, is class-biased, as tax filers who benefit the most tend to be the affluent who can most afford to give.

Like ordinary donors of cash, donors of publicly traded securities receive the income tax credit by claiming the market value of their donation. In addition, these donors receive tax savings from the lowered (now waived) capital gains tax of their appreciated assets. In this way, the policy of reducing (and then eliminating) capital gains tax amplified the regressive structure of the income tax credit by benefiting those who own shares over those with only cash to give. For regular monetary gifts, the donor's share of the gift is approximately 50% to 60%, depending on the province, whereas for gifts of securities, factoring in savings of capital gains tax, the donor's share is 40%, at most. To put it the other way, the tax subsidy of large gifts comprised of securities is at least 60% of the value of the gift (Standing Committee on Finance, 2013).

The regressive design of the charitable tax incentives may be justified if the philanthropy it stimulates is redistributive in its effects, if, in other words, people at lower income levels experience its benefits. However, tax expenditures in general, including the charitable income tax credit, lack transparency because the question of who benefits is difficult to answer and seldom investigated (Duff, 2003; Rushton, 2008). At the time of the 2001 decision to permanently halve the capital gains tax, effective 2002, little was known about how the increased gifts of publicly traded securities were spread among charities over the preceding four years, except that "a disproportionate amount of such gifts was received by larger charities, educational charities, and public foundations" (Philipps, 2003, p. 922). These were the type of recipient organizations that first employed Mavis until she went to work trying to increase the capacity of small charities to receive gifts of securities, that is, gifts that carry the largest tax subsidy.

Besides Mavis, my sample of 50 fundraisers included only one other self-employed fundraising consultant serving small charities. Ultimately, Mavis and those like her would have limited success in changing how the benefits of the tax expenditure tended to flow to large charities. Large charities such as universities have significant fundraising resources, including financial advice for benefactors about how to make the most of tax incentives. Such organizations can offer additional incentives for major philanthropy, including publicity, membership in elite circles, and access to exclusive audiences such as alumni or the organization's other patrons. A further regional bias arises in philanthropy because wealth tends to be concentrated in large urban centres (Reich, 2006). As donors typically give close to home, the charitable donation tax expenditure is weighted towards charities in high-income, urban neighbourhoods.

Tax incentives, as hidden subsidies that disproportionately benefit certain donors, types of charities, and locales, are difficult to debate when other policies for nonprofit sector support are not on the table (Duff, 2003). In the absence of policy alternatives, Mavis supported the new tax incentives, seeing them as the least way the federal government could compensate for cuts to social spending:

> The federal government has at least responded in terms of its tax policy. You know, they've created a lot more options for people to make philanthropic gifts, particularly larger gifts. So they have been very definite in their policy of trying to promote giving. So, at least, if they see the cutbacks on the one side, at least they haven't just walked away from the table. (Mavis)

Philipps (2003) offered further explanation for the charitable tax policy. At a time when markets were soaring, tax-avoidant constituencies of Canadian society were pressuring the government to reduce capital gains taxation: "While the prospect of reducing taxes for this group [Canada's wealthiest citizens] may be generally unpopular with the vast majority of Canadians, such an initiative may be rendered politically saleable if it is packaged in a way to finance charitable activities that benefit less-privileged citizens" (p. 924). The remainder of this chapter explores fundraisers' work to "package" this regressive tax policy along with a broader neoliberal programme under the rubric of fostering a culture of philanthropy.

Defining a Culture of Philanthropy

In addition to Mavis, several of the fundraisers I interviewed spoke of their political commitment, above and beyond their day jobs, to introduce a culture of philanthropy. For example, Leah, who had worked in three large fundraising departments within a university, hospital foundation, and arts organization over 18 years, told me, "My biggest soapbox [speech] is [about] making philanthropy a Canadian social norm." Other fundraisers, who located themselves across a spectrum of political identities, similarly used the interview as a soapbox to expound the need to cultivate philanthropic norms. Their arguments illustrated Nikolas Rose's (2000) analysis of the rhetorical shift from "society to community" accompanying the neoliberal transformation of welfare states (p. 1400).

Twentieth-century welfare states such as Canada have been described through various analytical lenses such as liberal-democratic, Fordist, Keynesian, regulatory, redistributive, and social states. However they are defined, welfare states were basically founded on promises of relatively stable conditions for corporate capitalist accumulation coupled with social protections against capitalism's worst harms. These protections included government provision of health care, education, and leisure opportunities, support for the arts and scientific research, environmental protections, insurance against unemployment, and basic supports for people whose age, health status, or care of dependents placed them outside labour markets. Critics of neoliberalism should not be tempted to romanticize welfare state arrangements, which depended on nuclear family forms, required the daily and intergenerational reproductive labour of women, and excluded or marginalized large groups of people by citizenship status, race, indigeneity, sexuality, and disability (see Braedley & Luxton, 2010). Nevertheless, welfare state arrangements, underpinned by progressive taxation, were hard-won results of social struggle. For a few decades after the twentieth-century world wars, as Rose (2000) put it, "[the welfare state's] image of social progress through civility, solidarity, and security won out over both the image of social revolution on one hand and that of unfettered competition on the other" (p. 1400).

The historic compromise between capitalist classes and revolutionary labour to provide social security in exchange for stable conditions for profit began to fail as the financial economy outstripped corporate capitalism. As Rose (2000) put it, replacing the image of the "welfare" state, we have, "the facilitating state, the enabling state, or the state as animator" (p. 1400). To put it differently, capitalism's neoliberal turn has shifted the state's priority to facilitating, enabling, and animating markets and quasi-markets.

Neoliberals cast the welfare state as a costly, inefficient, bureaucratic encumbrance to economic growth. They also discredited it on moral grounds as a restraint on competitiveness, the preeminent value of neoliberal regimes. Market mentalities and market solutions were deemed morally preferable to the dependency instilled by the state's excessive, misplaced generosity. In short, for neoliberals, the welfare state demoralized its beneficiaries, whereas competition spurred them on, sharpened their abilities, improved their performance, and fostered efficiency all-around (Dardot & Laval, 2013, p. 230). Even as waves of privatization and cutbacks widened social disparities along the lines of class, race, and gender, neoliberalism pushed a fierce moral critique of welfarism and evaded the age-old condemnation of market society as based in greed and exploitation.

As Rose (2000) observed, a shift in rhetoric from "society" to "community," marked the neoliberal transformation in welfare state politics:

> Populations that were once under the tutelage of the social state are to be set free to find their own destiny. Yet, at the same time, they are to be made responsible for their destiny and for that of society as a whole. Politics is to be returned to society itself, but no longer in a social form: in the form of individual morality, organizational responsibility, and ethical community. (Rose, 2000, p. 1400)

The hallmark of "government by community" would be personal caring, donating, and volunteering (Vrasti & Montsion, 2014, p. 340). As fundraisers spoke of "community," this hope animated their politics: that individual morality and community ethics could take the place of government social welfare.

Fundraisers' talk of creating a culture of philanthropy resounded with support for neoliberal values and policies. However, fundraisers' talk also exposed the continued tensions between neoliberalism and competing discourses. At times, the vision of a "culture of philanthropy" was constructed in opposition to welfarism. At other times, it seemed to awkwardly incorporate aspects of welfarism. As Woolford and Curran (2012) explain, "Neoliberals are not strict ideologues in the sense that neoliberalism has shown a remarkable capacity to borrow and redeploy the discourses, programs, techniques, and policies of other competing theories, blending them to fit a neoliberal agenda" (p. 54). Irrespective of occasional clashes or overlaps between neoliberalism and welfarism, even fundraisers who disagreed politically on the role of the social state and taxation found common ground on the need to promote philanthropy and to use tax incentives to do so.

Fundraisers' near-consensus across ideological differences also revealed that neoliberalism is suffused with paradox, as Wendy Brown (2015) has illustrated through the example of public-private partnerships. Public-private partnerships are complex, long-term arrangements for public infrastructure and service provision, which involve governments working with for-profit businesses and financers, and which typically require a substantial "local share" generated through philanthropic fundraising (Whiteside, 2016, p. 105). Brown writes: "[Neoliberalism] seeks to privatize every public enterprise, yet valorizes public-private partnerships that imbue the market with ethical potential and social responsibility and the public realm with market metrics" (p. 49). Public-private partnerships, or P3s, represent more than privatization; by blurring the lines between public and private, P3s turn profit-making into an overarching public good, which public and nonprofit partners jointly work to support.

Philanthrocapitalism, epitomized in P3s, further illustrates Brown's argument about paradox: that neoliberalism repudiates government and public morality, but at the same time relies upon them to advance market logics. The standard critiques of philanthropy apply also to philanthrocapitalism but on a new scale. If philanthropy is a strategy for individuals and families with extreme or ill-gotten wealth to rehabilitate their reputations by giving away some of their fortunes (Wagner, 2000), philanthrocapitalism performs this reputational rehabilitation for neoliberal capitalism itself. Premised on the "hyper-agency" of the ultra-rich and the discovery that markets-with-morals can facilitate business-as-usual, philanthrocapitalism is the attempt to reconcile social responsibility with continued accumulation and consumption (Bishop & Green, 2008; Vrasti & Montsion, 2014, p. 340).

Fundraisers obscured the political work of philanthrocapitalism by conflating philanthropy and charity. If charity seeks to meet an immediate need, and philanthropy aims for a lasting impact, philanthrocapitalism is a more entrepreneurial style of philanthropy that regards the gift as a strategic investment and seeks a "return" in terms of measurable results (see Special Report: Wealth and Philanthropy, 2006). However, for fundraisers, the "culture of philanthropy" seemed to refer to all donors—casual, monthly, annual, major givers, and venture philanthropists alike. All groups were deemed united in giving what they could, according to their means. This framing rightly acknowledged that the rich are not more generous than the poor when giving is evaluated as a percentage of income (Wagner, 2000). However, the notion that everyone can be a philanthropist erased the politics of wealth and inequality inherent in philanthropy, and especially in the turn to philanthrocapitalism. Ivan Drury (2014) made this point in an essay in *Briarpatch Magazine* about urban development in the city of Vancouver:

> Taking moral cues (but not policy) from social democracy, philanthrocapitalism aims to replace taxation and state-driven redistributions of wealth with voluntary acts of charity and "innovative" micro-market projects. To sell their charity as social change, philanthrocapitalist leadership draws on potent cultural symbols associated with social justice and sustainability, obscuring structures of inequality and exploitation.

In this way, philanthrocapitalism, "represents a friendly alternative to the ugliest aspects of capitalism" (Drury, 2014).

In the remainder of this chapter, I flesh out three aspects of the "Canadian social norm" of philanthropy that fundraisers sought to create. As Leah and her colleagues spoke about philanthrocapitalism and other philanthropic trends, they focused on three interrelated ideals: a widespread culture of philanthropy would instil an ethic of generosity; it would enshrine democracy; and it would transform social infrastructure in a positive direction. I have emphasized that not all fundraisers thought alike, but most interpreted these three ideals—generosity, democracy, and societal transformation—through market logic and in reaction to welfarism. To be specific, they defined generosity in opposition to paying taxes, painted philanthropy as democratic, and lauded major philanthropy as transformative, so long as that transformation was oriented towards investment, competitiveness, practices of calculating and maximizing outcomes, and entrepreneurialism. As Wendy Brown (2015) would say, fundraisers' pervasive economic rationality transferred the sphere of politics into the sphere of the market.

A Better Society Through Generosity: "Not Something That Can Be Left to Government"

At minimum, a "culture of philanthropy" for Canadian fundraisers referred to the ideal of making generosity widespread; it meant individuals voluntarily embracing expanded responsibility for the charitable entities of their choice. Vance said as much when he shared his impression that a culture of philanthropy was growing in Canada. Over his 16-year career working for an environmental NGO, an independent school, a university, and two hospital foundations, he claimed to have witnessed a shift in Canadian's attitudes:

> I think there's more of an understanding that we all have more of a role to play. [...] This is not something that can be left to social service organizations and government. That is, on an individual basis, we need to do what we can in regardless of what form, big donors, small donors, volunteerism, whatnot, to make Canada a better society. (Vance)

By equally problematizing reliance on government and social service organizations, which are largely state-funded, Vance voiced scepticism about the role of government as both a deliverer *and* a funder of social services. In this vision of the "culture of philanthropy," typical of the fundraisers in this study, societal betterment depended on voluntaristic giving—people donating what they can of their time and money. Vance welcomed the emerging understanding that "we all have more of a role to play" to compensate for shortcomings of social service organizations and government and fill a service void.

How is it that, for fundraisers like Vance, uncoordinated charitable acts, small and large, had the potential to "make Canada a better society" in ways that tax-funded programmes could not? I got insight into this question from my interview with Dawn, a major gifts fundraiser who had worked with two universities and a hospital foundation. I asked her whether tax policies to incentivize philanthropy shift some of the responsibility for social provision from government onto individuals. "Yes, I think, absolutely," she agreed, but promptly asserted that promoting philanthropy is important in itself as a moral project that remedies the welfare state's moral failings.

> It's interesting because I do believe though in a philanthropic culture. I do think that it makes individuals better and it makes a society better when people are philanthropic. (Dawn)

Fundraisers working in social welfare agencies did not necessarily hold stronger commitments to welfarism than their colleagues in charities less tied to state funding. For example, Sharlene's varied 16-year career had led her to an executive position with a national social service charity that served vulnerable populations. She had thought about the politics of philanthropy as someone who witnessed the effects of government cutbacks on her agency and its clients. In response to the question I posed to Dawn, she first referred to the Canadian political writer, John Ralston Saul.

> His [Saul's] position is that philanthropy is a very inefficient way to support community need.[3] And from a practical, tactical point of view, I see that side of it. The other part of me really does believe in the importance of community engagement and of people voluntarily giving some of what is theirs, and sharing, right? [...] I do think that that's a really important communal value in a society, that if you just leave it all to taxation, you're missing that whole thing that can create something quite lovely. (Sharlene)

In this remark, Sharlene's endorsement of welfarism acknowledged the "practical, tactical" advantages of state provisioning; however, she distinguished this pragmatic stance from her moral position, which advocated individualized generosity. Sharlene could have conceptualized taxation as "sharing" and as a "communal value" through a welfarist orientation but, typical of her colleagues, she spoke of philanthropy in contradistinction to taxation. Donating, not tax-paying, was morally improving of individuals and society for Sharlene, and so philanthropy has indispensable societal value, even when promoted at the expense of, admittedly more efficient, tax-funded social programmes.

While most fundraisers generally agreed with Sharlene on the moral necessity of philanthropy, their general views of taxation were conflicted. Representing one pole was Charles, who had headed capital campaigns in top fundraising positions, first for a university and then a consulting firm, over his 19-year career: "How much do people want to pay in tax to the government at the end of the day?" Charles asked rhetorically. "I think government should get out of the way in some ways. Be a strategic partner but let these [nonprofit] organizations develop themselves as well. Grow, thrive, succeed!" Supporting a platform of low taxation and few government-administered programmes, Charles argued that people would donate more only if government did less.

In contrast, Glenn, who identified as a social democrat, defended welfarism. Reflecting on his 16 years working for a disease-related health charity, social service organization, and hospital foundation, Glenn argued that tax-paying, like philanthropy, should feel important and meaningful:

> One of the arguments why philanthropy is so important [is] because it's a voluntary giving to a cause, and it can be redemptive, it can be meaningful. My hope would be that people also, to a degree, feel the same way about their taxes, that that [taxpaying] is an important thing that we [citizens] are doing as well. I think politicians do a bad job of making that case (laughing), and there are ideologies that are fully against that and are not trying to make the case. So that's a big fight as well in our society. (Glenn)

While Charles and Glenn appear to be far apart politically on the issue of taxation, they both positively evaluated their work as fundraisers against what they saw as a failure of government. When Glenn said, "I think politicians do a bad job of making that case [for taxation]" he implied that fundraisers do a superior job of what they call, "making the case for support." In a similar way, Charles argued that governments fail to perform the most basic, obligatory task of fundraisers: thanking donors in a personal way.

> If I make that donation to charity of $200, that's $100 that I can take off the taxes that I would pay to the Receiver General. I'm happy with that decision and I've done good for a community that I believe in. Salvation Army, Red Cross, Big Brothers and Sisters, whatever it is, YMCA, I'm going to support them and they're going to thank me. [But] I write a cheque for the government, they never thank me. You know, I bust my butt for them, you know, and I never get a thank you from the prime minister, the finance min-

> ister, in all the years that I've been doing it. So, you know, people are just fed up with it. And they want to do something that's good for their community. (Charles)

Charles' exhibition of "tax rage" (Patriquin, 2004), and his sympathy with the chauvinistic wishes of "fed up" people to benefit "their community" and not pay taxes, may seem polar opposite to Glenn's stance on the "big fight" for fair taxation, but these ideologically dissimilar fundraisers expressed common ground on the need to cultivate civic generosity. Like Vance, Dawn, and Sharlene, who emphasized the moral benefits of philanthropic culture, Charles and Glenn saw themselves as doing vital work that government was unwilling or unable to do. They all advanced a neoliberal culture of philanthropy by defining generosity in tension with tax-paying and by elevating the virtue of individual giving to make up for the insufficiency of tax-funded programmes.

Charitable Tax Incentives as Power to the People

Democracy was the second ideal I heard repeatedly associated with the goal of creating a culture of philanthropy. Democratic ideas arose especially in discussion of fundraisers' lobby for more tax incentives for charitable donations. In each interview, I explored views on the gradual augmentation of tax incentives over the years. Fundraisers held that the multiplication of major gifts in number and size, one of the most significant changes of their careers, was directly owed to these incentives, particularly the elimination of capital gains tax on donations of appreciated publicly traded securities. The success of the revised tax code in raising more and bigger major gifts made it patently good public policy.

To better understand the consensus on tax incentives, I introduced the objection that the tax credit for charitable donations was undemocratic because it allowed individuals to trigger a government subsidy in the form of a tax expenditure for the charities of their choice. In other words, individual whims would allocate money that would have gone into public coffers and been expended through a budget process. Tax incentives were also class and gender biased, I pointed out, in that they allow those who make the largest donations, disproportionately wealthy men, to trigger the largest government subsidy. If there were no statistical differences in who donates how much and where, tax incentives would be less objectionable, but differences exist. For instance, the tax expenditure assists hospitals, universities, and large cultural institutions, which are favoured by the richest donors, more than social service organizations and religious charities, which are the preferred causes of ordinary donors (Duff, 2001, p. 47).

Some fundraisers admitted to being unfamiliar with these arguments, saying they had regarded their professional organizations' advocacy of increased tax incentives as uncontroversial. In response to the challenge I raised, most backed the tax incentives on the grounds that they successfully stimulated major gifts, which were needed and would not happen otherwise. Interestingly, their defence of government-supported philanthropy was often framed in *democratic* terms. For example, Diane, whose 18 years' experience was with children's and disease charities and a large hospital foundation, justified the tax credit when I reminded her that large and mega-donors were, in effect, allocating the expenditure of "public money" because over half of the value of their donations would be returned to them as tax credits. Diane's response applied the language of popular sovereignty to multi-millionaires:

> I say it [the portion of the gift that is offset by the tax credit] is still public money. It's just that you're allowing the donor to choose where it goes versus it going into the pot and the government. You're putting power back into the peoples' hands. (Diane)

Diane's identification of philanthrocapitalists with "the people" illustrated Wendy Brown's (2005) argument that neoliberal governmentality (governing mentality) "resignifies democracy as ubiquitous entrepreneurialism," and as "thoroughgoing market rationality in state and society" (p. 50).

Another fundraiser of 15 years, Duncan, who had worked for a large Christian charity, as well as nonprofit organizations in the arts sector, took issue with the argument that the people who make the most use of the tax incentive have different value systems, material interests, and political priorities than the majority.

> I don't see the major gifts that I've encountered doing anything that would shift value systems or shift interests or shift priorities. I wonder if that's coming from an elitist approach thinking that, 'Well they're just giving 10 million to the opera and the opera only deals with the elite.' The thing is that I think that for many of these major gifts, the money wouldn't be coming in any other way. [...] People who say that are being a bit elitist thinking that major gift donors are going to wag the dog, the tail is going to wag the dog, and I don't agree with that. (Duncan)

Both Diane and Duncan's statements attempted to deny or reverse class hierarchy. In another instance of what Brown (2015) called "the language of democracy used against the demos" (p. 128), economic elites became "the people." People who challenge class privilege became "elitist."

Fundraisers' most common defence of the charitable income tax credit policy likened donating to the neoliberal touchstone of consumer sovereignty, "the economic power exercised by the preferences of consumers in a free market" (Merriam-Webster, n.d.). They argued that the free exercise of individual preferences in donating was akin to voting and an instantiation of democracy. For example, Elizabeth, whose 20-year career was with both small and large hospital foundations, a large arts organization, an independent school, and a national consulting firm, justified the tax-sheltering aspect of philanthropy saying, "Maybe that's okay, maybe that's a way of voting for certain causes, for what people believe in."

While analysing a different social policy (Canada's long-form census), sociologists William Ramp and Trevor Harrison (2012) described this analogy between everyday consumer activity (shopping or donating) and voting:

> If a commercial organization cannot continue to attract "votes" in the form of dollars freely offered, the argument goes, it has no right to patronage; indeed, no right to exist. By extension, this transmutes into a justification for neoliberal resistance to state intervention in the economy; to state provision of goods and services; to state "monopolies" in areas such as education and health care, and ultimately, to "mandatory" state interventions in private life or business that do not derive from some specific and freely expressed majority preference. (Ramp & Harrison, 2012, p. 284)

By the same logic, the charitable income tax credit was justified because it appears to organize state support for the charitable sector through a voluntaristic process, like shopping or voting, which appealed to neoliberal populism.

Charles, referred to earlier, illustrated a fundraiser's expression of neoliberal populism. As a service to the clients of his consulting firm, Charles created digital tools for charities to help donors calculate their tax savings. He argued that the tax system ought to reward donors (in his view, refrain from punishing them), and emphasized that donors have the right to support their selected charities with their own tax-exempt money:

> I just think that the people who've made the money and choose to share it, that's their prerogative. [...] And so by the very nature of having an opportunity, this is the democratic process. [...] You vote with your cheque book in this case. (Charles)

When I responded that, "Only a very few get to vote with their cheque book," suggesting that donating is more an exercise of economic power than a universal right, like voting, Charles disagreed. He maintained that donating is so widely practiced, and available to anyone, it is virtually a universal practice:[4]

> No, but 22 million people donate to charity every year. So, whether you're supporting somebody who is going to run for breast cancer, walk up the CN Tower, [whether somebody] goes to a gala, supports a cause, writes a cheque to whatever organizations that they want to, 22 million is the adult population. It's almost a hundred percent giving across the board. So, everybody votes. Everybody has the opportunity to participate. It's just not the elite. The elite happen to get their name on a building but the differentiation between the elite and the person who is the token donor to an organization, there's no difference. [...] The differentiation is the person who gave five million dollars, or ten or twenty million dollars, did it and has been recognized for it in a more public way. So, there is no, there's no issue. (Charles)

In arguing that "everybody votes" or has that opportunity, and "there's no difference" between six-figure philanthropists and people who sponsor a friend's charity bike ride, Charles transposed the principle of formal equality between citizen-electors into the neoliberal image of the market as the proper sphere of democratic politics. Both ordinary and mega-donors were equally valued contributors to charity in Charles' understanding and it was not relevant that the wealthiest philanthropists received the most attention of fundraisers, a disproportionate share of tax incentives, and the greatest opportunity to shape an emergent culture of philanthropy and the nonprofit and voluntary sector. In this way, neoliberal discourse performed a levelling operation in conjunction with another move that Ramp and Harrison (2012) called, "the consumerization of political rights [and] ... of politics itself" (p. 284). Through such discursive work, fundraisers such as Charles sought to align philanthropy with a particular interpretation of democratic values. In doing so they substantiated Brown's argument that neoliberalism is stealthily "undoing democracy" by "converting the distinctly *political* character, meaning and operation of democracy's constituent elements into *economic* ones" (Brown, 2015, p. 17, emphasis in original).

Transformative Philanthropy and the Business of Changing Lives

Societal change is the third ideal fundraisers associated with a "culture of philanthropy." Just as Todd, introduced in Chap. 1, described fundraising as "the business of hope," Myrna, a fundraising consultant for 23 years, similarly said, "We're in the business to change lives [...], you know, fundraisers, we're agents of change where money just happens to be the vehicle. It's all about changing lives." Tamara elaborated on this theme. Drawing on a 16-year career that started in a social service charity and transitioned to a national, multi-sector nonprofit network, she summed up fundraisers' purpose this way: "We are in the business of engaging citizens actively in the life of their community over a period of time in ways that have transformative potential." Each of these fundraisers compared themselves to salespeople marketing hope to prospective donors that a gift of money could change lives and communities for the better.

Most fundraisers also boasted a distinctly neoliberal brand to their business: self- and community-entrepreneurship. They made clear that the old welfarist brand of hope, whatever its merits or flaws, had been retired. For example, Darlene, who had developed many fundraising specializations in her work with a hospital foundation over 20 years, reiterated the neoliberal axiom that there is no alternative to devolving responsibility for personal and civic wellbeing to individuals when she said: "I mean the government, it just simply can't be everything to everybody. And we have to embrace as humans what we can do for our own wellbeing."

The job of many of the fundraisers I interviewed was to pitch hope for social change primarily to potential major donors, ideally those with philanthrocapitalist mindsets and extraordinary net worth. For example, Leah, who expressed the populist-sounding aspiration to "make philanthropy a Canadian social norm," later described the emerging trend towards "transformative philanthropy," another term for philanthrocapitalism, which Drury (2014) has also referred to as the charity of the super-rich with, "the discursive sparkle of social change":

> A lot of the transformational gifts are gifts that will affect [...] public policy. So, a lot of the large gifts are really looking to address very significant needs within society. [...] It's [become] that much more strategic, where I [the philanthrocapitalist] see a problem in society that needs to be fixed and I recognize that a million dollars isn't going to do it. We need a $30 million gift to do it because we need the buy-in from all parties and I need to be a big player in it. (Leah)

In this business of changing lives by helping mega-donors strategically solve social problems, fundraisers needed to establish the political legitimacy of major philanthropic interventions. In the interviews, I heard them apply two criteria, one an explicit, professional standard, the other a taken-for-granted political logic, when deliberating on whether to support donors' strategic use of wealth. First, they considered whether the terms of the gift were consistent with established priorities. Fundraisers' ethical practice required that their solicitations correctly reflected the recipient organization's mission.[5] They took seriously this professional mandate to help donors match their personal philanthropic goals with organizations' greatest needs without causing "mission drift," which Mavis explained as follows:

> Donors want to be engaged, they want to be involved. So, there are some repercussions to that. I mean, that can create a tension within an organization between [pause], well, some people would refer to it as "mission drift," if you get donors who are, kind of, calling the tune. You know, if you've got a big donor who is walking up with $5 million but they have their own particular vision, that's great, as long as that coincides with the vision of the organization. But does it skew things? (Mavis)

To Mavis' rhetorical question, after resolving concerns about "mission drift," did donors' influence on organizations "skew things," a second, more implicit criterion came into play. The political legitimacy of transformative gifts depended on the type of politics they advanced. Gifts were acceptable when the change they proposed appeared to be market-driven, and therefore, supposedly outside the scope of the political. Elizabeth (cited earlier) spoke this tacit rule aloud during a discussion of small charities' disadvantages compared to those with big fundraising shops:

> Unfortunately, I think that the mean, lean, fundraising-machine organizations [...] they really get a huge, huge percent [of overall donations] versus

> something like the food bank that probably is really, really important in society in general. And, in fact, a contribution a similar size to what a big university might get would have a huge impact, probably even too big of an impact. It would change the dynamics of it. So, I'm a believer in letting the market do what it should when it comes to fundraising. (Elizabeth)

Elizabeth rejected the idea of soliciting gifts on the order of tens of millions, such as large universities occasionally receive, for food banks. Funding of this magnitude would change the dynamics of food banks, potentially reducing hunger and increasing food security to the point that the food bank mission of providing short-term emergency rations was no longer needed. For Elizabeth, this would be, "too big of an impact." Instead, allocating wealth to social needs was best left to a "market" in which philanthropic opportunities compete. Elizabeth recognized the vital work of small charities but ruled out rectifying their inequality. As Wendy Brown (2015) explained, "Inequality is the premise and outcome of competition. Consequently, when the political rationality of neoliberalism is fully realized, when market principles are extended to every sphere, inequality becomes legitimate, even normative, in every sphere" (p. 64).

Elizabeth's example of the food bank revealed the neoliberal standard for transformative philanthropy: social inequality and its consequences, such as hunger and food insecurity, were not to be transformed. Rather, competition—in particular, the uneven competition among charitable organizations to land major gifts—was to arbitrate the political questions of transformative philanthropy. So long as philanthrocapitalists were perceived as players in a market, and their gifts reinforced market mentalities involving innovation, evaluation, investment, and entrepreneurialism, they could operate as change-makers. Likewise, when fundraisers represented themselves as responsive businesspeople, they could exercise their political agency in doing the work of neoliberalization: transforming political, moral, and ethical spheres along the model of markets.

Fundraisers' Political Agency

Fundraisers in the 1990s and early 2000s, in response to the urgent needs of de-funded nonprofit organizations, set themselves the ambition to develop a culture of philanthropy. In doing so, they made themselves agents of neoliberalization. Working through professional associations, they successfully advocated overhauling tax rules to promote philanthrocapitalism, the highest expression of the culture of philanthropy. They were rewarded by career mobility across organizations and up the ranks in a growing industry centred on soliciting major gifts. Their advocacy helped consolidate the renegotiated relationship between the state and nonprofit organizations that I described in Chap. 2, which threw charities into intensified competition for donors and entrenched the fundraising industry in Canada's political economy. In the conduct of their jobs, the establishment of their careers, and the work of their associations, fundraisers instilled a philanthropic culture according to the same neoliberal rationality of economization that guided the programme of reduced social spending.

Fundraisers circulated legitimizing discourses of neoliberalism as they defined the culture of philanthropy in particular ways. Specifically, they presented a moral vision of philanthropy as a vehicle for generosity, democracy, and social transformation. Their individual ideological differences did not seem to affect the coherence of this vision, as they consistently represented philanthropy as an alternative to tax-funded social programmes. They understood generosity as individual giving and as antithetical to taxation. They cast plutocratic activity and donor-centrism in the egalitarian language of liberal democracy, and peddled hope for social change, with the proviso that change must be along a neoliberal trajectory that maintains social inequalities, and with the parallel message that there is no alternative.

Notes

1. Witnesses at the hearings represented the Association of Fundraising Professionals, Canadian Association of Gift Planners, Canadian Council of Christian Charities, Council for Business and the Arts in Canada, Health Charities Coalition of Canada, Canadian Centre for Philanthropy (now Imagine Canada), and Philanthropic Foundations Canada, as well as large charities such as the National Arts Centre Foundation and Ducks Unlimited.
2. With the introduction of a higher top marginal tax rate in 2016, the portion of a donation exceeding $200,000 qualified for a charitable income tax credit at the rate of 33%.
3. Sharlene associated John Ralston Saul's critique of charity with concern over "inefficiency," a neoliberal fixation. In fact, Saul focused on how charity buttresses class privilege and weakens democracy, as indicated in this quintessential quotation about signs that "concepts of democracy and citizenship are weakening": "There is an increase in the role of charity and in the wor-

ship of volunteerism. These represent the élite citizen's imitation of noblesse oblige; that is, of pretending to be aristocrats or oligarchs, as opposed to being citizens" (Saul, 1998, p. 468).

4. Charles is correct that a large majority of Canadians give to charity but not everyone does, and higher-income donors contribute much more than most. According to the General Social Survey, 85% of respondents said they made a charitable donation in 2004, dropping to 82% in 2013 (Turcotte, 2015). However, the most reliable data for showing trends in donation rates comes from income tax records. In 1990, 29.5% of Canadians claimed charitable donations when filing income taxes. From that high point, the number of tax filers with receipted donations dropped by more than a third by 2014 (Lasby & Barr, 2018). By 2019, less than a fifth of tax filers (19%) reported a charitable donation. In 2019, Canadians with incomes above $150,000 made up 10% of donors but this high-income group accounted for 41.7% of the dollar amount of all donations (Statistics Canada, 2022).
5. See Association of Fundraising Professionals (n.d.) AFP Code of Ethical Standards. https://afpglobal.org/ethicsmain/code-ethical-standards

References

Association of Fundraising Professionals. (n.d.). AFP Code of Ethical Standards. https://afpglobal.org/ethicsmain/code-ethical-standards

Bishop, M., & Green, M. (2008). *Philanthrocapitalism: How the Rich Can Save the World*. Bloomsbury Press.

Braedley, S., & Luxton, M. (Eds.). (2010). *Neoliberalism and Everyday Life*. McGill-Queen's University Press.

Brown, W. (2005). Neoliberalism and the End of Liberal Democracy. In W. Brown (Ed.), *Edgework: Critical Essays on Knowledge and Politics* (pp. 37–59). Princeton University Press.

Brown, W. (2015). *Undoing the Demos: Neoliberalism's Stealth Revolution*. Zone Books.

Dalby, P. (2003, May 8). Will the 'Me Generation' Become Generous Givers? Many Will Be Inheriting Part of About $550 Billion; Charities Hope People Will Plan Their Donations. *Toronto Star*, p. K.04.

Dardot, P. & Laval, C. (2013). *The New Way of the World: On Neoliberal Society*. Verso Books.

Drury, I. (2014, September 1). The Rise of Philanthrocapitalism: What Passes for Progressive City Politics Today. *Briarpatch Magazine*. https://briarpatch-magazine.com/articles/view/the-rise-of-philanthrocapitalism

Duff, D. G. (2001). Charitable Contributions and the Personal Income Tax: Evaluating the Canadian Credit. In J. Phillips, B. Chapman, & D. Stevens (Eds.), *Between State and Market: Essays on Charities Law and Policy in Canada*. McGill-Queen's University Press.

Duff, D. G. (2003). Special Federal Tax Assistance for Charitable Donations of Publicly Traded Securities: A Tax Expenditure Analysis. *Canadian Tax Journal, 51*(2), 925–936.

Fennell, T., Walmsley, A., & Allen, G.. (1990, November 5). A Trillion Dollar Windfall: Baby Boomers Will Inherit Tremendous Wealth in the Next 20 Years, Leading to a Big Spending Increase. *MacLean's*, 48–52.

Lasby, D., & Barr, C. (2018). *30 Years of Giving in Canada: The Giving Behaviour of Canadians: Who Gives, How, and Why?* Rideau Hall Foundation and Imagine Canada. https://imaginecanada.ca/sites/default/files/2019-05/30years_report_en.pdf

Merriam-Webster. (n.d.). Consumer Sovereignty. In *Merriam-Webster.com Dictionary*. https://www.merriam-webster.com/dictionary/consumer_sovereignty

Patriquin, L. (2004). *Inventing Tax Rage: Misinformation in the National Post*. Fernwood Publishing.

Philipps, L. (2003). Thinking Critically about the Taxation of Capital Gains on Donated Public Securities (or looking Paragraph 38(a.1) in the mouth). *Canadian Tax Journal, 51*(2), 913–924.

Ramp, W., & Harrison, T. W. (2012). Libertarian Populism, Neoliberal Rationality and the Mandatory Long-Form Census: Implications for Sociology. *Canadian Journal of Sociology, 37*(3), 273–294.

Reich, R. (2006). Philanthropy and Its Uneasy Relation to Equality. In W. Damon & S. Verducci (Eds.), *Taking Philanthropy Seriously: Beyond Noble Intentions to Responsible Giving* (pp. 27–49). Indiana University Press.

Rose, N. (2000). Community, Citizenship, and the Third Way. *American Behavioral Scientist, 43*(9), 1395–1411. https://doi.org/10.1177/00027640021955955

Rushton, M. (2008). Who Pays? Who Benefits? Who Decides? *Journal of Cultural Economics, 32*(4), 293–300.

Saul, J. R. (1998). *Reflections of a Siamese Twin: Canada at the End of the Twentieth Century*. Viking.

Special Report: Wealth and Philanthropy. (2006, February 23). The Birth of Philanthrocapitalism: The Leading New Philanthropists See Themselves as Social Investors. *The Economist*. http://www.economist.com/node/5517656

Standing Committee on Finance. (2013). *Tax Incentives for Charitable Giving in Canada. James Rajotte, Chair. 41st Parliament, 1st Session*. House of Commons. http://www.ourcommons.ca/DocumentViewer/en/41-1/FINA/report-15

Standing Senate Committee on Banking, Trade and Commerce. (2004). *The Public Good and Private Funds: The Federal Tax Treatment of Charitable Giving by Individuals and Corporations*. Interim Report. Jerahmiel S. Grafstein, and W. David Angus, Chairs. Senate of Canada. https://sencanada.ca/Content/SEN/Committee/381/bank/rep/rep04dec04-e.pdf

Statistics Canada. (2022). *The Daily, Charitable Donors, 2020.* https://www150.statcan.gc.ca/n1/en/daily-quotidien/220412/dq220412d-eng.pdf?st=BDZSUMoP

Turcotte, M. (2015). Charitable Giving by Individuals. Spotlight on Canadians: Results from the General Social Survey. Statistics Canada. http://www.statcan.gc.ca/pub/89-652-x/89-652-x2015008-eng.pdf

Vrasti, W., & Montsion, J. M. (2014). No Good Deed Goes Unrewarded: The Values/Virtues of Transnational Volunteerism in Neoliberal Capital. *Global Society, 28*(3), 336–355.

Wagner, D. (2000). *What's Love Got to Do with It: A Critical Look at American Charity.* New Press.

Whiteside, H. (2016). *Public-Private Partnerships.* Fernwood Publishing.

Woolford, A., & Curran, A. (2012). Community Positions, Neoliberal Dispositions: Managing Nonprofit Social Services within the Bureaucratic Field. *Critical Sociology, 39*(1), 45–63.

CHAPTER 4

Living for Philanthropy: Fundraising as a Vocation

Abstract This chapter explores the meaning fundraisers give to their work. For the first wave of Canadian fundraising executives and consultants, fundraising was not merely a job or career but a vocation. Many wished to make their mark by raising money for worthy causes and contributing to a caring capitalism, an economic system that combines investor profit and social responsibility. The most donor-centric of fundraisers also found a calling to spiritually enrich major donors. Only 1 fundraiser of the 50 I interviewed fashioned a vocation that supported political action of social movement organizations. The political subjectivity of this singular fundraiser and her uneasy relationship to her profession illustrates how the neoliberal rationality of this period, though pervasive, was not universal.

Keywords Vocation • Caring capitalism • Donor-centric fundraising • Spiritual growth • Social movements

In the late 1980s, Ruby, an administrative assistant for a travel agency, responded to a newspaper ad for a telethon secretary at a children's hospital foundation. This would be her entry point into a stellar fundraising career. "I fell into [fundraising] by accident," she reflected, "which I think is pretty common for people who have been in this industry for as long as I have." She did not know of any of her contemporaries who set out to

M.-B. Raddon, *The Business of Hope*, Palgrave Studies in Third Sector Research, https://doi.org/10.1007/978-3-031-18837-4_4

work as fundraisers. "It really is only recently that I've seen people start to choose fundraising as a career coming out of high school or university," she observed.

In this chapter, I consider the extraordinary career trajectories of Ruby's cohort of Canadian fundraisers who were excelling at their work through the 1990s and the years leading up to the global financial crisis of 2008. Drawing on their interviews, I describe how Ruby and 49 of her peers understand their work as meaningful to them beyond other jobs or careers they may have had. As other research with fundraisers has found, the participants in this study viewed their work as a vocation to better society (Breeze, 2017).

In 1905, Max Weber showed how the notion of a secular calling became widespread among European Protestants in tandem with the rising spirit of capitalism in the sixteenth century. I am interested in exploring how twenty-first-century fundraisers similarly embraced their work as a vocation: "the valuation of the fulfilment of duty in worldly affairs as the highest form which the moral activity of the individual could assume" (Weber, 1958, p. 80).

My conversations with fundraisers showed that not all interpreted their vocation in the same way. Some sought to affect change by helping institutions achieve their mission. These vocational orientations often reinforced neoliberalism by normalizing and depoliticizing the reconfigured relationships among governments, nonprofit organizations, citizens, and business elites that gained momentum in the 1990s. Some fundraisers primarily sought to change individuals. This group spoke of their work in quasi-religious terms about a mission to help wealthy people become more spiritually fulfilled by practicing generosity. The effect of this vocational rationale, beyond legitimizing economic inequality, was to sanctify the mega-philanthropy that neoliberalism was making possible.

Only one of the fundraisers whom I interviewed, Vivian, created a vocation to change society through grassroots fundraising for social movement organizations contributing to human rights and environmental justice. Her story illustrated the difference between neoliberal and social justice-oriented discourses of social responsibility. Vivian's willingness to take political action, not only through her fundraising causes but also in the way she conducted herself as a fundraiser, brought her into conflict with colleagues, a conflict that highlighted the dominant conception among fundraisers of what it meant to do good in the world.

Accidental Careers

The fundraisers interviewed for this study began their careers in the mid-1970s through the mid-1990s, but most, like Ruby, began in the late 1980s when fundraising was still a new occupation. Most had another career before fundraising. Only 19 of the 50 participants were introduced to fundraising as a component of their first job. Nine of these launched their fundraising careers starting as university students working part-time in the Advancement office, soliciting donations from alumni over the telephone among other jobs. None of the 50 claimed to have had an early life ambition to become a professional fundraiser. Even among those whose first job involved fundraising, few embarked on the work as a consciously chosen career. On the contrary, whether fundraising was a first job or a job switch, most participants spoke of "falling into fundraising" or starting the career "by accident."

If Ruby's "accidental" start in fundraising was typical of her generation, so too was her soaring career trajectory, which eventually made her vice president of a national consulting firm:

> So, I was there [with the hospital foundation] for 13 years and rose through the ranks, and when I left, I was Director of Corporate Major Gifts within the organization. So, within a 13-year period I went from a secretary to a director position, which was phenomenal because, to be honest, one of the reasons I had looked to make a change with my previous employer was because I was pigeon-holed as a secretary and was having a hard time trying to get out of that hole within the confines of the organization I worked for. (Ruby)

Sharon similarly started out in an unfulfilling career with no prospects for advancement. Realizing she was going nowhere professionally, she changed course and accepted a position with an established social service organization. Within 19 years of her switch, she was head-hunted into her fourth fundraising role, a top-level executive position for one of Canada's largest hospital foundations. She described how the demand for fundraisers came about at the time when she was gaining experience.

> [The first organization I worked at] has been the training ground for lots of senior fundraisers because, that many years ago, that was 1990, there weren't nearly as many charities fundraising. The government was still covering lots

> of costs. [...] And you know, quite frankly, even universities were starting, but hospitals, many hospitals weren't really actively fundraising yet. (Sharon)

As Chap. 2 details, the fundraising industry expanded in the years following cuts to transfer payments from the federal to provincial governments. As successive governments restructured social spending, nonprofit and voluntary organizations needed to ramp up fundraising. Designated fundraising positions and fundraising consultant work emerged as job opportunities just as public and private sector careers were being eroded by the double whammy of government cutbacks and recession in the early 1990s.

Glenn, for instance, identified fundraising as an occupation only after training and practicing as a social worker. His graduation with a Master of Social Work coincided with the imposition of Ontario's "Common Sense Revolution," a radical neoliberal programme of cutbacks to social services.

> My intention was to go into the community organizing side of social work but Mike Harris [Ontario Premier, 1995-2002] had just to come to power and there were all kinds of cuts to social services and so there wasn't a lot out there. But through information interviews, I learned about fundraising, that it was a profession. And the more I learned about it, the more I thought, wow, this sounds very interesting because it's very relationship-oriented, you're working for a cause, it's entrepreneurial, it's creative, so it seemed like a good fit for me. (Glenn)

As fundraising career paths opened before them, and these early entrants gained traction, Ruby, Sharon, Glenn, and others came to consider their seemingly accidental work as a vocation. Ruby was not alone in feeling that, "it was like it was meant-to-be." Like many of her peers, she transformed her unforeseen entry into fundraising into a mission-filled expression of her life's work.

Falling into a Vocation

These career stories align with Beth Breeze's research with U.K. fundraisers about the nature of their occupation. In *The New Fundraisers, Who Organises Charitable Giving in Contemporary Society* (2017), Breeze found the vast majority of her interview respondents regarded their work as "more than a job" that pays the bills but a calling to make positive change (p. 173). Unprompted, fundraisers spoke of the satisfaction they derived from doing work that makes a difference in the world.

The generation of successful Canadian fundraisers whom I interviewed, identified many ways their work felt satisfying: earning what many thought a good living, achieving career mobility, excelling at the technical aspects of their jobs, enjoying the pace and variety of the work, the challenge of meeting goals, and the pleasure of cultivating relationships. Even so, for most, fundraising was much more than a decent job and a good career choice.

These consistent findings that successful fundraisers view their work as a calling are not surprising. Acting on a sense of vocation as a fundraiser may actually propel career success (see Breeze, 2017, p. 173). Participants in my study made this point emphatically: when required to serve as a spokesperson for an organization's mission, it helps to believe in that mission. For example, a senior fundraiser of 25 years, Ken argued that to be a successful fundraiser, you must "have a genuine and sincere interest in people and in the organization that you're serving, a belief in its mission, its purpose, what it's trying to accomplish to make society a better place." Ken lamented the frequency of fundraisers "flitting around," by serving a charity for two years before moving on to "the place across the street" for a "25% salary increase." Another fundraiser, Bruce, worked for five organizations over 17 years, and claimed, "Whatever you are doing, you have to be really passionate about the cause." Perhaps feeling susceptible to the kind of critique levelled by Ken in relation to frequently moving jobs for higher pay, Bruce added, "I think you just have to believe, also, on a more personal level, that you have a mission to create a better world. You have to really believe in doing that and making a difference."

Believing they were following a calling was also a way for fundraisers to mitigate the stress of the work. As many pointed out, in this line of work failure is visible and quantifiable. Working as the only fundraiser, or as one of only a few staff, could be especially nerve-wracking when the continuity of programmes, services, and other staff members' jobs depended upon meeting annual targets. In larger organizations, toxic work environments, so called poisoned shops, were not uncommon, according to my participants. Despite these stressors, Michael, a veteran fundraiser of 34 years, typified the vocational attitude when he said: "I don't want to ever think of myself as living off of philanthropy but living *for* philanthropy."[1]

Ways of Living for Philanthropy

As fundraisers constructed their vocation, they worked with and against clashing public images reflecting neoliberal culture. On the one hand, fundraisers could be regarded as heroic because they brought needed money to organizations that had been starved under neoliberal restructuring and austerity. Fundraisers were seen as mitigating the harshest effects of neoliberal policies by helping the nonprofit sector fill a role that had been undermined or vacated by government. Whether they were organizing mass participation events or brokering multimillion-dollar donations, they were champions who helped their organizations thrive in hard times.

On the other hand, neoliberal rationality of value-for-money placed fundraisers under scrutiny. Was their work effective and efficient? What were the costs of fundraising and what percentage of donations went towards overhead, including their own salaries? Fundraisers faced suspicion about the value of their jobs and whether they were benefitting unduly from the generosity of donors. Fundraisers in large organizations needed to establish their legitimacy against neoliberal denigration of bureaucrats in quasi-governmental workplaces. Those in smaller organizations, especially women, struggled against the notion that charitable work should be performed by volunteers or receive a low wage.

As I listened to fundraisers, it turned out that "living for philanthropy" meant different things. All fundraisers wanted to affect positive change, but vocational priorities fell into three tendencies: the desire to change specific institutions and locales for the better, to change individuals for the better, and to support movements for social and environmental justice. The third, least common, mission contrasted with the neoliberal rationalities evident in the first two.

Building a Caring Capitalism

The first, most typical way fundraisers were called to make change was by working through their nonprofit agencies to support worthy goals. Fundraisers' work brought about tangible results, enabling institutions and programmes to better serve people and communities. For example, Ken pointed out the ways he had contributed to his city over his 25-year career:

> I look around this community […] and I can say, 'I helped facilitate that new building at the hospital. I helped ensure that renovation of that theatre. I helped create that new art gallery. I helped build […] endowed funds for student aid that wasn't there before I helped.' So, I can look around and see the results, but none of those things has my name on it. It's all the result of facilitating those things for donors […]. The donor's name is on those things often. I just know that those things just wouldn't have happened without our involvement in some way to facilitate things. So that's hugely satisfying. (Ken)

Ken's satisfaction in his career success typifies the first sense of fundraising as vocation: facilitating work that makes a positive difference to people or their communities by supporting organizations' infrastructure or programmes.

Some of the scholarship of neoliberalism makes it difficult to recognize Ken and other fundraisers as neoliberal subjects in the fashioning of such moral vocations. Simon Springer's (2016) anatomy of neoliberalism, for example, emphasizes neoliberalism as violence. Springer argues that neoliberal discourses have material effects which perpetuate colonialism, dispossession, violence, inequality, and poverty. He goes further to vilify neoliberals as greedy, selfish, and uncaring:

> By refusing to confront the inequality, poverty and violence of its own making, neoliberals console themselves by happily looking not at cause and effect, but only to their own accumulation of wealth. It is a discourse that perpetuates and even actively promotes utter and extreme selfishness. But the true believers of neoliberalism have proceeded as though we are all none the wiser. … They simply don't care. … Can't we admit that sometimes it is crucial to appreciate the common good? Neoliberalism refuses this, where any notion of collectivity is dismissed and demonized. (Springer, 2016, p. 134–6)

Fundraisers and the philanthropists they court complicate and contradict Springer's argument that selfish "neoliberals" do not care about the common good. In all likelihood, they do care.

Neoliberalism refers to the extension of market rationality into non-market spheres of life, including social morality (Dardot & Laval, 2013). The problem and perversity of neoliberalism is that it institutes a "caring capitalism" that redefines what it means to care in market terms. Emily Barman's (2016) book by this title examines various fields in which markets and social values are intentionally entwined, including nonprofit organizations, social enterprises, socially responsible investing, corporate social responsibility, responsible investments, inclusive business, and impact investing. In these fields, "value entrepreneurs" define and measure social value in complex ways to establish the moral underpinning of economic enterprises.

The most commonplace of fundraisers' vocations for social change, as exemplified by Ken, is inflected by a market orientation that seeks to do good by means of individual choice, competition among service providers, and striving to achieve value for money. Under caring capitalism, fundraisers construct what it means to care and to be generous as an individual, private matter. To such an orientation, the threat to social morality is not individual self-interest, or even selfishness or greed, but universal, tax-funded social programmes delivered by the state and provided as a social entitlement to all citizens.

Dardot and Laval (2013) argue that, for neoliberals, the welfare state is deemed costly to society not only in financial terms but also because it "demoralizes," which is to say, the state is thought to remove the impetus for individuals' moral behaviour:

> According to a number of [neoliberal] polemicists, it is on the moral terrain that public action [of the state] can have the most negative effects. More precisely, it is on account of the demoralization that it risks creating in the population that the policy of the 'welfare state' has become especially costly. This major theme of neo-liberalism has it that the bureaucratic state destroys the virtues of civil society—honesty, the sense of a job well done, personal effort, civility and patriotism. ... It is the state that undermines the springs of individual morality. (Dardot & Laval, 2013, p. 164)

Ken's fundraising career illustrates how caring capitalism was pitted against the welfare state. Ken developed his fundraising forte in planned giving from a background in financial planning, which gave him technical financial knowledge: "that sense of understanding structured instruments, working with life insurance, gifts of securities, remainder trusts, gifts of annuities." He warned that unless our financial wealth is planned, it will be subjected to taxes upon death (probate fees, capital gains, and income taxes):

> Unless we choose to influence how we'd like to see it [capital] invested in society, it will be invested by government. We tend to talk facetiously, in the

> planned giving world, about 'inherit a new child,' a charity of your choice and disinherit the government by taking action during one's lifetime. (Ken)

The notion of "disinheriting the government" is the epitome of a neoliberal worldview that grounds social morality in personal choice and pins hope for social change on individual agency. The fundraiser's mission of raising "voluntary income," as opposed to coerced taxes to fund social programmes, lowers expectations of the role of government (Breeze & Scaife, 2015, p. 592). Ken's dismissal of government denies that tax-funded, democratically organized, politically determined state forms of social provisioning could also be an expression of social morality. In contrast, Ken allies himself with caring capitalists who glow in the virtue of giving and revel at paying as little tax as possible.

Changing the World by Changing Donors' Hearts

Along with the commonsensical understanding of fundraising as advancing good work for worthy causes, fundraisers expressed another, more specific, calling: to cultivate and facilitate donors' philanthropic ambitions. Indeed, the most frequent response to my question of what makes their work satisfying was the pleasure of working with donors. Consider, for example, how Duncan extolled the donors to the major arts organization, religious charity, and other nonprofits for which he had worked over 15 years:

> [These donors were] some of the most outstanding individuals and examples of humanity that I've ever met. And I'm so grateful for the opportunity to meet them, to be enriched by them emotionally, to see their gifts go to an organization where they feel strongly about how they're making a difference. It's very, very satisfying. (Duncan)

This sense of satisfaction fuelled a vocation to change the world by changing wealthy individuals. Darlene illustrated this donor-centric career orientation as she reflected on her 20 years with a large hospital foundation:

> What I am able to take home at the end of the day is the deep sense of satisfaction *that a donor has* for being able to do what they've done. [...] There's lots of studies out there about how good it makes people feel to give and I think it's definitely true. I've seen people's faces light up in ways that

> I didn't know was possible. [...] That would be something that I strive for on a day-to-day basis, is to bring that sense of gratification to our donors. And if that is working, then I'm feeling fulfilled. (Darlene, emphasis added)

In a concrete way, Darlene's work served the hospital foundation, but her primary sense of vocation was in making donors feel good. Such donor-centrism was identified as a new trend over this period, as Mavis explained based on her experience as a fundraising consultant in planned giving:

> One of the trends that you see happening that they talk about in the sector now is, quote, *the new donor*. And how the new donor is different than, you know, (voice trails). And when I talk about donors, I'm thinking about major donors. So once upon a time, a wealthy person would write a cheque and give it to an organization and get their thank you and that would basically be it. Whereas the new donor, it's all about, you have to be donor centered. We have to meet the, quote, *needs* of our donors. (Mavis)

Whether donor centrism originated with a changing generation of donors, as Mavis suggested, or in new fundraising practices, it had become a significant approach in raising major gifts. A fundraising manual by Carl W. Davis, *Because Donors Want to Share* (2015), underscored just how far this trend had gone by the mid-2010s to upend traditional approaches. Fundraisers, and the nonprofits that employed them, were not serving clients, wrote Davis, they are primarily serving donors: "Nonprofit organizations exist as conduits for charitable minded individuals to accomplish their personal philanthropic goals" (p. 1). Such a donor-centred orientation allowed Sharon, cited earlier in this chapter, to reflect: "I don't feel like I'm asking people for money. I feel like I'm helping them accomplish something important and showing them the opportunities." To a strongly donor-centric way of thinking, the purpose of fundraising is to help donors experience their wealth as agency. As Davis put it:

> Our nonprofit agencies exist as tools for donors to use to bring their dreams to fruition. It makes sense to call a nonprofit organization an agency because it is an agent of the donor's philanthropy. (Davis, 2015, p. 2)

Donors' realization of agency in giving could be a powerfully emotional experience for fundraisers themselves, who witnessed major gift decisions. For example, Gary, who had worked with a social services agency, a university, two national disease charities, and a national consulting firm in his 19-year fundraising career, described the experience and its significance:

Gary:	I've been with a few donors in my career where you're actually there when they change. They literally transform right in front of you.
Interviewer:	What's that like?
Gary:	Well, it's an adrenaline rush for you, and for them, they're literally taking another step up towards self-actualization. And that's what it's really about.

Gary tied philanthropic agency to transformative spiritual growth. Changing donors' lives was core to how he and fundraisers like him defined their vocation.

Gary's enthusiasm to facilitate donors' spiritual growth is reflected in a subset of fundraising manuals written for the staff of Christian religious charities, including leaders of church congregations, but also Christian parachurch organizations such as religious schools, chaplaincy programmes, religious outreach programmes, and charitable social services. For these authors and their readers, Christian fundraising constitutes a ministry that is not reducible to utilitarian goals of soliciting contributions to Christian causes. This approach epitomizes donor-centrism because it makes donors' spiritual growth fundraisers' foremost priority. For example, the authors of *Growing Givers' Hearts: Treating Fundraising as Ministry* (Jeavons & Basinger, 2000), compared fundraising as ministry with traditional fundraising:

> [In fundraising as ministry,] relationships with donors should be built around the desire to spur their spiritual growth. The ethical baseline is more proactive and less minimalistic. It makes doing good for the donor a primary concern rather than either a side benefit or a "selling point" to entice the prospect. (p. 4)

Celebrated Catholic theologian, Henri Nouwen (2010), similarly argued that fundraising must be good for the donor, not only the recipient. This stance goes beyond teaching religious precepts and practices related to generosity such as tithing; Christian fundraisers have a calling to facilitate a *conversion* experience for donors as a result of their philanthropy.

> In fundraising as ministry, … we want them [donors] to experience that they will in fact benefit by making their resources available to us. We truly believe that if their gift is good only for us who receive, it is not fundraising in the spiritual sense. Fundraising from the point of view of the gospel says to people: 'I will take your money and invest it in this vision only if it is good for your spiritual journey, only if it is good for your spiritual health.' In other words, we are calling them to an experience of conversion. (Nouwen, 2010, pp. 19–20)

Only one of the fundraisers in my study worked for a Christian church foundation, but several expressed non-sectarian versions of this idea of fundraising as promoting spiritual growth and conversion. For example, this was how Elaine, a fundraiser of 16 years, described her passion and purpose:

> Fundraising is about […] creating those meaningful exchanges where donors feel, 'Not only am I creating change, I'm experiencing a personal change because of my act of generosity.' That spirit of our work as fundraisers is critically important. […] So in terms of my own passion and commitment for the work of philanthropy, for me, that's where it is. (Elaine)

Gary, cited earlier, expressed this vocational orientation the most emphatically. Drawing on popular understandings of Buddhism, he recounted the thrill of witnessing moments when donors attained "philanthropic enlightenment":

> If the fundraiser is doing their job, the person [donor] really feels the difference that they're making. So, it's no longer they're supporting you. It's that they're creating a difference in the world and they're supporting something much larger than themselves. So, it's taking them away from themselves into, again, Buddhist enlightenment is the closest parallel that I can think there might be. They change. They *change*. (Gary)

The vocation to change people for the better through individual major gift philanthropy has similar political implications to caring capitalism. The perceived opposite of fundraising, social provisioning through taxation, would eliminate the prospect of helping to impart the aura of enlightenment on the philanthropic class. Fundraisers want to contribute to societal change as well as individual betterment, and they see these goals as connected through cultivating generosity. The threat to generosity is comprehensive state provisioning, which would take away these conversion opportunities.

A Vocation for Social Justice

As neoliberal social and economic policy paved the way for the fundraising profession, fundraisers tended to adopt a corresponding political rationality. However, neoliberal subjectivity was never universal. Competing moral and political frameworks remained available, as Vivian's uncommon case reveals.

Vivian described her start in fundraising much like her peers: "Many people like me in the '80s fell into it," she said. Her "fall" started with a part-time job that had a fundraising component while she was training in a different field. Upon entering her first full-time fundraising job, "It was like, 'Oh my God!' (laughing) I was totally hooked because I *got* it." She dropped her original career plans in favour of a new role in a health charity where she was the only fundraiser on staff. Here she said she was expected to run a capital campaign, start an annual giving programme, and independently do, "everything, from meet with bank presidents to send receipts and thank-you letters." She took fundraising courses in the evenings and attended annual conferences to learn from more senior fundraisers.

After two years, in the late 1980s, Vivian went to work for a large international humanitarian NGO. After five years, she was head-hunted to a second international NGO and seven years later, a third. I met her a decade later, when her combined fundraising experience of over 24 years included 16 years as a national fundraising director. Reflecting on her career, she explained that early on she'd had, "that sense that, 'Okay, this is what I'm supposed to do!'" Like other fundraisers, she said of her work, "It felt like a vocation." Unlike others, however, she went on to specify her vocation as working for social change through collective, political avenues: "It felt like, this is something I can do [well] and this is something I can do for social movements."

Vivian's commitment to environmental justice and human rights was the foundation of her career, but she found that practicing her political values as a fundraiser sometimes put her at odds with professional colleagues. "I have a complicated relationship with the profession," she told me, laughing, but continued in a serious tone: "Because I love being a fundraiser, and I think this [profession] is some of the best of our society, in this sector. But I also think it's some of the worst masquerading as some of the best."

One way Vivian stood apart from her peers was in being selective about where she worked. Once she had her start, she chose organizations that she had previously supported as a donor, member, or volunteer. Her respect for these agencies' politics and personnel led her to want to stay on over the years, despite the lure of higher salaries elsewhere. "I get head-hunted a lot," she confided. "I see lots of other jobs and they just don't have the same appeal, but this [current job] feels very compelling."

From time to time, friends in the field expressed surprise that she had not yet traded up for a more lucrative salary at another charity, as was common for fundraisers after 18 months to 2 years, she explained. At one point, persistent questioning from others led her to question herself. Was there "something wrong with me?" she asked. Did she lack career ambition? Did she undervalue her talent? Was she selling herself short? Ultimately, she dismissed these doubts but not without soul-searching. "Once I realized that I didn't want my epitaph to be, 'She earned as much as she could,' I was *fine* with not making more money," she said. She committed to staying on with an agency she admired, leading a staff team she liked, and doing work she intrinsically loved. Prioritizing mission over money concretely exemplified the ideal of living for, not off, philanthropy.

Another thing that distinguished Vivian from others who claimed fundraising as a vocation was her relationship to donors. She was far from donor-centric in the ways her peers emphasized. In part, she did not need to adopt donor-centrism as a fundraising method; her workplace relied on small, monthly donations from a broad member base rather than on soliciting mega-gifts of capital for buildings, major projects, or endowed funds. Broad-based giving was the type of fundraising Vivian preferred in principle because it circumvented reliance on the rich, which she argued, drew out the worst tendencies in fundraisers. "There is something appalling about our adulation of the rich as a profession," she started, and went on:

> Many fundraisers wish they were rich. We have this fascination with the rich. And I say we, inclusively, in that I'm a fundraiser, but I don't share that

> fascination (laughing). [...] Many people in the profession either feel that they *should* be rich, that they are *entitled* to be of the rich, or they really *love* the rich, or they want to hobnob with the rich. There is this kind of fascination, and 'what the rich do is good,' sort of notion. And many, many charities are just propping up the status quo. (Vivian)

Following Vivian's logic, the problem with adulating the rich was just this: many of the donors who commanded fundraisers' attention were not actually interested in world-changing causes. As a result, fundraisers seeking to change the world were limited to advancing the kinds of charities towards which wealthy donors gravitate. Vivian explained with an example:

> A lot of what we do, especially at universities, is endowing a chair in commerce in a school of management creating MBAs. It's very much *not* about changing society. There are parts of universities that do change society, but it [philanthropy] is very much about reinforcing the status quo. And many charities do that. We do it with our structures, the rich boards, and the way we deal with things. (Vivian)

The way fundraisers "deal with things" referred to the kind of donor-centrism to which Vivian most objected:

> There is something about the profession that props up the wealthy, in *all sorts* of ways, and admires the wealthy and says the wealthy are good. You trickle down some of your donations down to us and, 'Oh that's great, and you're a good philanthropist.' And we'll give you all sorts of awards and do all sorts of things that I don't subscribe to. (Vivian)

Vivian made her politics visible in fundraising circles. On one memorable occasion near the start of her career, she attended an international conference of the National Society of Fund-Raising Executives (NSFRE, now Association of Fundraising Professionals) in Chicago, where delegates witnessed the Award for Outstanding Corporation presented to Shell Oil Company. The year was 1995, and Shell Oil was facing intense protest campaigns, locally and internationally, over its documented environmental and human rights abuses in the Niger Delta. At the time of the conference, the writer and activist, Ken Saro-Wiwa, and eight other Nigerian land defenders were imprisoned, awaiting execution by hanging. Shell Oil was implicated in the false testimony at their trials and international condemnation was mounting (Ezeonu, 2018). Yet this was the year the NSFRE named Shell Oil Company "Outstanding Corporation" in a move that stunned Vivian:

> There are all sorts of reasons you could campaign against Shell because they're not good corporate citizens on all sorts of levels, but *especially* right now, they are complicit in the persecution of the Ogoni people, [in a region where] secret police are killing people. It's a terrible international travesty. (Vivian)

In response to the award announcement, Vivian and a few colleagues mounted a protest by leafletting, not merely boycotting, the awards banquet:

> Not going to the dinner was not enough. So, we did these little leaflets, and we put them at all the plates at dinner. And it was just a Shell logo with oil dripping down like blood, basically, and what their record was in Nigeria. (Vivian)

The icy response to what Vivian considered a mild protest struck at the heart of her disaffection with the profession:

> Of course, that [protest] was considered something that was 'not done.' You are not supposed to (voice trails off; switches to mimicking her critics)—'These are good people, with money. We're letting them whitewash their money through our charities, so how dare you raise the fact that they're killing people in Africa. And nobody cares about Africa anyway.' And all that sort of stuff. And I know it was 'not done' and I'm usually a well-behaved person, but we were *disgusted* with our profession. This goes beyond having a disagreement. (Vivian)

Many years later, Vivian remained appalled that the award decision came about, "just because they'd given some money to some place in Texas who had nominated them," despite the controversy surrounding the corporation. "We're shameful at times," she said, in a fervent rebuff to fundraisers' claims of caring about social issues, "we just don't care about that stuff."

Since then, Vivian has remained ambivalent about the profession:

> I want to be proud. You're supposed to be proud of your profession, and I am proud to be a fundraiser. I think what we do is great, but I think a lot of people [...] think that having money in itself is some kind of virtue. And too much of our profession is that way. There's actually very few of us that don't think that the world is structured the way it should be (pause), that the poor shouldn't have to rely on handouts. Very few of us actually think that. (Vivian)

Fundraising can be an appealing line of work, according to Vivian, because she and her peers "get to call ourselves one of the good guys." Yet, for those interested in changing the world, the project of cultivating virtue in individual donors through a kind of ethical makeover cannot replace the slow work of fundraising to sustain the campaigns of social movement organizations. A rare member of her profession, Vivian exposed her peers' vocations as invested in a mode of world-changing work that deepens the tracks carved by neoliberal movements towards caring capitalism. She also rejected the project of spiritually empowering a more agentic donor class.

The Limits of a Vocation to Fundraise

The growth of fundraising careers in Canada was more than a marker of neoliberalism. Fundraisers also participated in neoliberalization in ways they constructed as a vocation. Social theorist Wendy Brown (2015) wrote that prior to neoliberalism, the functions of government and business within the capitalist state were more distinct. Neoliberalism brought about a merger that saw governments more actively partnering with business in making economic growth and national economic health their common goals. At the same time, under caring capitalism, business increasingly took on civic goals, such as education, ethics, and inclusion, that had been the conventional domain of government. The emerging fundraising industry, by downplaying the social role of government and giving more prominence to an activist business class, contributed to this inversion of roles, where "government prioritizes economic growth, credit ratings, and global economic positioning while business represents the interests of the needy or underserved" (Brown, 2015, p. 149).

Fundraisers with a vocation for social change were limited in the kinds of change they could accomplish when they defined their mission as helping elite donors achieve their philanthropic goals. For example, expert advisor Carl Davis (2015) wrote in support of donor-centric fundraising:

"Donors give to the need they want to meet. They give to make the world look the way they want it to look, to be the way they want it to be" (p. 2). Donors may be interested in exercising power like that of government to determine social priorities, demonstrating their social responsibility as caring capitalists. However, they seldom want to change the social conditions of the world that placed them atop the donor pyramid.

Vivian's singular example shows an alternative vision for world-changing work. She dedicated herself to fundraising for organizations that fiercely challenged both government and business arms of the neoliberal capitalist state. This calling to social and environmental justice positioned her at odds with much of the fundraising profession, and yet she was able to use fundraising skills towards radical world-changing priorities that ranged outside of the neoliberal change efforts of her contemporaries.

Note

1. Michael's statement is a paraphrase of a line from Max Weber's essay "Politics as a Vocation" (1972).

References

Barman, E. (2016). *Caring Capitalism: The Meaning and Measure of Social Value*. Cambridge University Press.

Breeze, B. (2017). *The New Fundraisers: Who Organises Charitable Giving in Contemporary Society?* Policy Press.

Breeze, B., & Scaife, W. (2015). Encouraging Generosity: The Practice and Organization of Fund-Raising Across Nations. In P. Wieping & F. Handy (Eds.), *The Palgrave Handbook of Global Philanthropy* (pp. 570–596). Palgrave Macmillan.

Brown, W. (2015). *Undoing the Demos: Neoliberalism's Stealth Revolution*. Zone Books.

Dardot, P., & Laval, C. (2013). *The New Way of the World: On Neoliberal Society* (G. Elliott, Trans.). Verso.

Davis, C. W. (2015). *Because Donors Want to Share: A Donor-Centric Approach to Fundraising*. Blunderbuss Books.

Ezeonu, I. (2018). *Market Criminology: State-Corporate Crime in the Petroleum Extraction Industry*. Routledge.

Jeavons, T. H., & Basinger, R. B. (2000). *Growing Givers' Hearts: Treating Fundraising as Ministry*. Jossey-Bass Publishers.

Nouwen, H. J. M. (2010). *A Spirituality of Fundraising*. Upper Room Books.

Springer, S. (2016). *The Discourse of Neoliberalism: An Anatomy of a Powerful Idea*. Rowman and Littlefield International.

Weber, M. (1958 [1905]). *The Protestant Ethic and the Spirit of Capitalism* (T. Parsons, Trans.). Scribner.

Weber, M. (1972). *Politics as a Vocation* (H. H. Gerth & C. W. Mills, Trans.). Fortress Press.

CHAPTER 5

A Generosity Gap? Comparisons with the United States

Abstract This chapter examines changes in Canadian discourse on the relative generosity of Canadians and Americans. In the welfare era, public generosity through tax-funded programmes was a source of national pride, as Canadians boasted higher levels of collective provisioning for health, education, social welfare, and the arts compared to the United States. In the late 1990s, Canadians began to be reminded that we fall below the U.S. on measures of private generosity. Whereas at one time, the political left referred to Canada's "social advantage" over the U.S., now the political right pointed to a "generosity gap" based on Canada's lower rates and levels of charitable giving.

Keywords Generosity • Canadian national identity • Crowding out • Tax expenditures • Economic lag theory

Canadians famously derive our national identity by contrasting our institutions and values with those of the United States (see Michael Adams, 2009). Given this tendency, during the sea change of welfare state restructuring in the 1990s and early 2000s, Canadian fundraisers could not help but look to the U.S. and make comparisons. For example, after ten years of fundraising for environmental causes, Allison took on work as an independent consultant, giving her more opportunity to work in the United

M.-B. Raddon, *The Business of Hope*, Palgrave Studies in Third Sector Research, https://doi.org/10.1007/978-3-031-18837-4_5

States. Approximately half her clients were American environmental non-profit organizations, which she travelled to support. This cross-border experience led her to see the two fundraising contexts as different: "For me it seems like the U.S. is—what's the right word?—almost, like, *ahead of us* in terms of their fundraising programs and the way they fundraise and the way that donors work with them." She attributed Canada's fundraising lag to differences in the welfare state: "Probably because they [Americans] don't have the same government support, so they've always had to be more oriented towards private sector giving and towards building big endowments and just having a more ambitious attitude towards fundraising."

Over time, Allison noticed Canadian fundraisers starting to adopt these ambitious American approaches as they were increasingly inspired by the amounts being raised south of the border: "The [Canadian] groups that I work with, they are getting more and more willing to be ambitious and to work with individual donors and to ask for large gifts and be more (pause) direct (laughs) in their fundraising." However, Allison doubted that fundraising approaches in the two countries would ever converge, saying, "I think we're still pretty different than the United States."

This theme of Canadian fundraisers wanting to emulate their American peers despite the perceived and actual structural differences between the two countries recurred in my conversations. How Canadian fundraisers evaluated these national differences ranged. For some, the state of fundraising in Canada was evaluated neutrally, if not positively, whereas others pressed the need to Americanize. These assessments reflected fundraisers' political values, which responded to wider neoliberal cultural shifts.

The Generosity Gap

As success in fundraising is tied to generosity, fundraisers were intrigued by the question of which country exhibits greater generosity. Historically, this question has hinged on how generosity is defined. In post-war Canada, the political left asserted that Canada was the more generous nation on account of Canada's more comprehensive social safety net, publicly funded universal medical insurance, and public support of education, the arts, and other social institutions. This soft nationalist stance cemented support for policies of income redistribution through tax-funded, state-run social programmes. As those policies were dismantled in the 1980s and 1990s, Canada's positive self-image along these lines weakened. By the mid-1990s, arguments about Canada having a "social advantage" relative to the U.S. no longer held. Cuts to social spending at all levels of government reduced the public sector by about one-fifth within a few years and shrank the percentage of social programme spending relative to GDP by one-quarter (Stanford, 1998).[1] Economist Jim Stanford explained how these changes diminished Canadians' claims to being a generous society based on the relative public generosity of the Canadian state.

> It is hard to imagine how Canada's reputation as a 'kinder, gentler' society will be sustained. Even relative to the United States, the real role of government in our economy is shrinking dramatically: In 1992 total government program spending as a share of GDP was two-thirds higher in Canada than in the United States, but by 1998 this 'social advantage' would shrink to barely one-quarter. (Stanford, 1998, p. 45)

As Canada's public generosity was called into question due to public sector restructuring and cuts to direct government expenditure on social programmes, the political right began to shine a spotlight on Canadians' private generosity compared to the United States. This new analysis of generosity revealed Canadians to be *less* generous than Americans in terms of individual charitable behaviour. In other words, the leftist conception of generosity as a collective attribute, observable on the national level in the form of social programmes, was replaced by an individualized definition of generosity as personal charitable giving and volunteering.

The term "generosity gap" originated with the Fraser Institute, a neoliberal think tank, which took on the project of comparing charitable giving in Canada and the United States. Starting in 1999, the Fraser Institute issued annual reports called the *Private Charitable Generosity Index* (Clemens & Samida, 1999). Using data from income tax filers in both countries, these reports calculated an index of generosity for both countries and for each Canadian province and territory and each U.S. state, where "generosity" referred to personal tax-receipted donations to registered charities. The index was composed of two measures: the percent of tax filers reporting charitable donations (the "extent" of generosity) and the percent of aggregate personal incomes donated to charity (the "depth" of generosity).

The *Generosity Index* consistently revealed a "substantial generosity gap" between Canada and the U.S. (Gainer et al., 2008). Authors of the 2008 Index, for example, using data from 2006 tax records, found that approximately 5% more American tax filers reported a donation (29.7% in the U.S. compared to 24.7% in Canada), and the percent of aggregate income that Americans donated to charity was just over double that of Canadians (1.66% compared to 0.76%). Based on these findings, the report concluded that "private monetary generosity in Canada is considerably lower than in the United States. This generosity gap limits the power and potential of charities to improve the quality of life in Canada" (p. 9).

Early editions of the *Generosity Index* set out to confront the idea that public generosity is a legitimate basis for a positive Canadian self-image:

> A common perception, widely held by many Canadians, is that Canada is a kinder, gentler society than is the United States. In debates over social policy, for instance, the size and scope of Canada's welfare state is often used as an indicator of our more compassionate and generous nature. (LeRoy et al., 2002, p. 13)

Redefining generosity as personal monetary donations and revealing that Canadians, on the aggregate, are less charitable than Americans would have been less shaming if the Fraser Institute had offered more points of international comparison. A report by Imagine Canada and the Rideau Hall Foundation (Lasby & Barr, 2018), with data from the Charities Aid Foundation, compared levels of individual charitable giving as a percentage of gross domestic product (GDP). American charitable donations amounted to 1.44% of the national GDP in 2016, which was the highest donation rate among developed economies in the world. Canada ranked third on this measure, collectively donating 0.77% of GDP, well below the U.S., but only slightly behind second-ranked New Zealand (0.79%) and well above Australia (0.67%), the United Kingdom (0.59%), and all other large economies of Europe and Asia. Omitting this wider international perspective and the complexity it reveals, the Fraser Institute inferred that the Canadian charitable sector would be almost $10 billion richer, if only Canadian social policy came to mirror that of the U.S. (Gainer et al., 2008, p. 4).

Even prior to the first *Generosity Index*, members of Canada's business elite began to argue that private charity ought to replace the welfare role of government. Take Hal Jackman, the former Ontario Lieutenant Governor, whose name has appeared on Canadian Business magazine's list of the 100 wealthiest Canadians since the practice started in 1998. In 1997, Jackman delivered a speech to the Canadian Club that justified cuts of $500 million in government grants to the nonprofit sector on the grounds that the withdrawal of government funding would motivate Canadians to be as generous as Americans (Jackman, 1997). Noting that Americans give almost three times more of their taxable income to charity than Canadians, Jackson attributed this difference to Canadians having "too high expectations of government." Pointing to a mythologized settler colony which had "no roads, no schools, no hospitals, no government services of any kind," he imagined that "our [European] ancestors survived because they accepted responsibility to look after each other." The presumed lack of state provision for these ancestors imbued in them a "spirit of community and citizenship" that Jackman warned we were "in danger of losing." Government spending was to blame for suppressing personal generosity, as comparison with the U.S. supposedly revealed: "There is a hidden cost to large government programs—because it is obviously apparent that there is a strong correlation between government support and the lack of private-sector support" (Jackman, 1997).

Jackman went on to argue that Canada was bound to regain the "essence of citizenship which defines us as a nation" through renewed volunteering and donating, "once our citizens know there is no big government there to do it for us." In the 1980s, arguments for cutbacks revolved around the idea that government belt-tightening was imperative to achieve deficit reduction. However, Jackman speaking in the late 1990s turned government retrenchment into a moral creed. He advocated reducing government social spending as a national strategy to get Canadians, "back to that spirit of community which nourished us during our formative years."

How Fundraisers Interpret the Generosity Gap

When I first asked Canadian fundraisers to identify significant trends in both fundraising and philanthropy, comparisons with the U.S. arose frequently. When comparisons were not mentioned spontaneously, I raised the question for any trends they had mentioned. Many of the responses touched on perceived cultural differences. American donors were described as more generous, open about money, and accustomed to and accepting of fundraising. Americans were seen as stronger boosters of their hometowns and colleges, and their attitudes of "give back," "can-do," and stalwart self-reliance made them more loyal givers to particular causes. Canadian donors, in contrast, were described as more "polite," "cautious," and "conservative" in their reception to fundraising appeals. Canadian fundraisers considered their American colleagues as more "confident," "ambitious," "assertive," "aggressive," "sophisticated," and "competitive." They saw their own kind as "docile," "nice people," "soft," and "delicate" in their approach to fundraising.

Beyond these cultural observations, many fundraisers offered sociological analyses as they sought to understand and take practical lessons from differences in levels of charitable activity. Important explanations for the "generosity gap" were advanced, such as Americans having more vehicles for philanthropic giving and more opportunity for tax filers to report the monetary value of small in-kind donations.

Differences in religiosity were cited as another explanation, given that regular religious attendance is positively correlated with charitable activity and the largest amounts of charitable donations go to religious organizations (Turcotte, 2015). Religious donations have been declining in Canada since 1969, especially in Quebec, which ranks lowest of the provinces on the Fraser Institute's *Generosity Index*. For Canada as a whole, between 1969 and 1997 the proportion of households that made charitable donations declined from 78% to 73% (Reed, 2001). According to Reed (2001), this drop, "was due mostly to a marked drop in donations to religious organizations..., from 74% to 64% of total charitable contributions. Both the incidence of donating to religious organizations and the total amount donated to them has declined." Religiosity in the U.S., although declining, is considerably higher than in Canada (see Pew Research Center, 2019, p. 14; Cornelissen, 2021).

Some fundraisers also drew attention to another basic factor in the generosity gap: the difference in the wealth structure of the two economies. The highest-income groups donate at the highest rates and make the largest donations (Lasby & Barr, 2018). It is worth mentioning in this discussion of generosity, that Canadians with low and moderate incomes donate more as a percentage of their pre-tax household income compared to high-income households (Hall et al., 2009). As income is closely correlated with wealth, it follows that the U.S. has a greater capacity for philanthropy given the higher number of billionaires per capita and the greater magnitude of fortunes of the ultra-rich compared to Canada. Consider that in Canada in 2010, the share of total net wealth owned by the top 10% of households was 50%, whereas in the U.S., the top decile owned 77% of total net wealth (OECD.stat, 2021). Of the top 1% in Canada, the share of total net wealth was 15.5% but 37% in the U.S. Comparisons of personal generosity as a national trait need to take into consideration that the most significant American donor classes have vastly more wealth to give.[2]

Expectations of Government

One of the most common explanations for the generosity gap was differences in the structure of the welfare state, as Allison's comments above illustrate. A university fundraiser, Larry, took Allison's reflections a step further by presenting a strategic avenue for fundraising that follows from the "generosity gap" analysis. Reflecting on his 16 years in charge of Advancement for one of Canada's largest comprehensive universities, Larry identified the biggest change he saw in his career as a shift in the goals of university campaigns: "Our last campaign, we talked about raising money for 'excellence,' for 'the differences,' for 'the cream' type of thing. Now it's a lot more about raising money for basics, for almost day-to-day operations." He interpreted the change as reflecting a shift in Canadians' perception of the welfare state: "I think the realization is that we are no longer, kind of, a totally socialist country, that our taxes don't pay for everything, and that we've got to start paying for things in other ways. And I think philanthropy is one of those ways."

The United States provided the counterpoint for his analysis starting with the observation that fundraising in Canada

> is very different from how it is in the States, where people in the States, you know, Americans are used to paying for everything. So, very quickly they realize that their philanthropic contributions are an integral part of that, and the government is not going to provide everything for everybody. (Larry)

This was a common argument. Decisions to give are based on donors' assumptions about need, which in turn are formed by assumptions about the responsibilities of government. Another fundraiser, Sean, with 19 years' experience working with a health charity, consulting firm, hospital foundation, and environmental charity, put it this way:

> Obviously, we're far more of a socialist society than the U.S. is, and I think our charitable giving on a per capita basis is still significantly less than in the U.S. Part of that is probably because of our expectations of the provision of services by the government. (Sean)

Larry's university set out to capitalize on the assumption that lowered expectations of government would increase peoples' willingness to give. "I think people are aware, especially if they read the paper, that the higher education sector is being cut back," he said. Accordingly, his university's new campaign for the "basics" instead of the "cream" counted on donors' concern about how reduced government funding threatened to diminish what universities could offer.

If more private giving was the desired response to the loss of public revenue, government cutbacks also provided an impetus to pursue privatization as an end goal. Larry explained that the university was soliciting prospective donors to contribute to its endowment so the interest on these invested assets could do more than fund scholarships and research chairs. Larry's vision was that the endowment could reduce the university's reliance on government grants for operating expenses:

> One of the pitches we always make is that it would be really nice to be independent from government funding and that's why we want to build up our endowment. So that's a long-term goal to have a buffer there. Now our endowment is growing and has grown substantially over the years. Part of the campaign will be to grow it even more and to be like the Harvards and the Stanfords with huge endowments so that you can sustain your program. (Larry)

The obstacle to attaining such growth, according to Larry, was cultural: "In the States, it's culturally very different," with the biggest difference being American graduates' active commitment to their *alma mater*.

> If you go to school in the States, you graduate with the idea that someone paid for me to be there, I'm going to have to pay for other people to be there, a kind of 'give back' attitude. Students come out with that idea already planted. (Larry)

Consequently, compared to Canadian fundraising campaigns, "their [American] participation rates tend to be higher, their engagement of alumni and just the whole relationship of alumni with their university I think is very different."

Larry envied the scale of fundraising the American alumni relationship enabled: "There are huge campaigns that have just finished in the States or are ongoing in the States with numbers like three billion dollars, three-and-a-half billion dollars, so they are huge!" Canadian university fundraisers were trying to inculcate an attitude of giving back, he said, by impressing this expectation on recent alumni. The message is slow to catch on, however, because "it's not a message their parents heard if they went to university either. So, it's not something they are hearing all the time."

Larry lamented that universities did not serve students well in the era of rapid expansion of higher education in the 1970s and 1980s when, "we turned into a bit of a factory for students." In the new millennium, Canadian universities began transforming their relationship to students to cultivate loyalty, such as American students show. Increased emphasis on varsity sports has been part of the new approach, but the broader strategy, according to Larry, revolves around, "recognizing that students are, they're our customer. Well, not customer, I don't like to use that [word] in an academic setting, but we really have to treat them well because if we don't treat them well, they're not going to treat us well down the road."

Only a few fundraisers in this study were in a position such as Larry's to contemplate the privatization of a university, hospital, or other largely publicly funded institution by cultivating relatively affluent students, patients, clients, or arts patrons as future donors. Government funding of the nonprofit sector in the early 2000s accounted for 51% of revenue, with fees and sales of services providing 39%, and philanthropy only 9% (Hall et al., 2005). Excluding universities, colleges, and hospitals from this overview, the largest source of nonprofit sector revenues was fees and sales (48%), followed by government funding (39%) and philanthropy (12%). Social services organizations were the most government-dependent sub-sector, counting primarily on government funding (66%), cost-recovery measures such as fees (23%) and philanthropy (11%) (Hall et al., 2005).[3] Assuming a nonprofit organization received revenues in approximately these proportions (50% government, 10% individuals' donations, and 1% corporate philanthropy), every cutback in government funding by a mere 1% for such an organization would require 5% growth in fundraising revenues or a 50% increase in corporate philanthropy to cover the shortfall (Evans et al., 2005). These funding arrangements have been relatively stable over time and demonstrate that fundraising could not replace the contributions of government without enormous change, including disruption to services (Hall & Reed, 1998).[4]

A Discourse of Inevitability

Many fundraisers, including those who appreciated the social role of government, interpreted Canadians' lower donation rates as being on course to eventually catch up to the United States. This way of interpreting difference, known as economic lag theory, suggests a linear course of change in which the U.S. sets the standard for Canadian developments. Frances, a fundraiser for a social services charity, community foundation, university, and hospital foundation with 25 years' experience, put it in this way:

> I think we're probably five to 10 years behind the U.S. and that many of the changes that are being seen in Canada now started in the U.S. five or 10 years ago. (Frances)

It is unsurprising that many Canadian trends originate in the United States given that fundraising techniques and models of best practice were passed along through joint educational programmes, conferences, professional organizations, accreditation agencies, and other forms of cross-border affiliation and exchange. However, developmental ideas that the U.S. was "ahead of" Canada, and Canada was "maturing," "evolving," or "making progress" in the direction of American fundraising interpreted the U.S. as the singular model towards which Canada was moving.

Some fundraisers also compared Canada with the U.K., Australia, and European countries. Samantha, for instance, president of an international consulting company, who had fundraised in three countries over 12 years, said of the U.K.: "They also have the government crutch as Canada has. They're starting to break out of that." Using selective cross-national comparisons to infer a trade-off between public provision and private philanthropy, Samantha and others were convinced of the inevitability of Canada's neoliberalization.

The Crowding Out Thesis

"Crowding out" refers to the idea that government social spending inhibits personal philanthropy. The most fully developed version of this idea posits an inverse relationship between government social spending and levels of charity: as the social state grows, people donate less; only as the social state recedes, will people step up to meet needs not addressed by government. In a rebuttal of the "crowding out" thesis, tax policy scholar Neil Brooks (2001) argues that the relationship between government action and private giving is statistically positive: "The neo-conservatives have it backwards," he contends. "The weight of the evidence is that public generosity aids and encourages private generosity" (Brooks, 2001, p. 190). Brooks points to countries such as Japan, which has a small public sector yet little private philanthropy. The historical evidence within Canada of government and nonprofit integration offers another refutation of the crowding out thesis.

The relationship of government to the nonprofit sector in Canada has long been interdependent, with taxation for social spending growing at pace with responses to charitable appeals. Historian Shirley Tillotson's (2008) study of Community Chests (United Way/Centraide) from 1920 to 1966 shows that broad appeal fundraising expanded in tandem with support for the welfare state and for paying taxes. Tillotson argues that the fundraising campaigns of the community chest movement paved the way for income tax policies, as the fundraisers and welfare state advocates made parallel arguments about the importance of collective provision. The "culture of contribution," wrote Tillotson, was "the common moral and conceptual framework that links taxation and charity" (p. 21). The twentieth-century advocates of taxation and charity did not see a contradiction between both ways through which citizens could answer social needs.

Another example of uniting philanthropic largess, fundraising, and advocacy for taxes was John Wilson McConnell (b. 1877, d. 1963). McConnell was a newspaper publisher and investor. As one of the wealthiest Canadians in the 1920s, he practiced philanthropy in the tradition of Andrew Carnegie and John D. Rockefeller (Wooster, 2009). He founded Canada's second private grant-making foundation in 1937, which remained the largest until 2000. McConnell's philanthropic giving in the fields of religion, education, and medicine grew in the 1920s and continued throughout his life. His major beneficiaries included the United Church, McGill University, and hospitals in Montreal (Fong, 2008).

As a Methodist, McConnell belonged to a tradition that promoted and practiced "systematic giving," a doctrine that dated from 1882. Systematic giving to missions and the church extended to fundraising campaigns among co-religionists and then the wider community, such as the Montreal YMCA campaign of 1909. McConnell's commitment to methodical giving dovetailed with his support for income tax and drove his successful lobby for a restaurant tax in Quebec, which was thought to be the model and precedent of Quebec's welfare system (Fong, 2008). As these examples indicate, there is not a necessary trade-off between tax-supported social spending by government and charitable giving. At least in the twentieth-century welfare era in Canada, taxation and philanthropy were understood as joint political objectives and not in opposition.

Comparisons of the Tax Subsidy of Philanthropy

The neoliberal formula of "less government, more charity" conceals the degree to which philanthropy depends on government support of the charitable sector in the provision of tax incentives for philanthropy. The fundraisers I interviewed frequently compared Canada to the U.S. with respect to the tax treatment of charitable donations. Most fundraisers perceived the U.S. as having more generous tax incentives. As Diane, a major gifts fundraiser for a hospital foundation, argued:

> When I say that we don't have as many tax incentives as the States has, we don't. They still have even more. … They get so many incentives for donors. Why do you think Harvard and Yale have a gazillion dollar endowment fund? Because they had those incentives there. (Diane)

In fact, the differences between the two tax systems are complex, starting with the differences between the American's estate tax and Canadians' capital gains tax. After lobbying by members of fundraising boards, representatives of financial institutions, and nonprofit sector leaders, the charitable tax credit has greatly expanded since the mid-1990s. By 2004, tax scholars and officials in the Department of Finance maintained that Canada's incentives for philanthropy were at least comparable to those in the U.S., and perhaps more extensive (*Proceedings of the Standing Senate Committee on Banking, Trade and Commerce: Issues Dealing with Charitable Giving in Canada*, 2004).

The charitable tax credit has a cost to government in terms of foregone revenue. Specifically, in 2008, the projected foregone revenue for the charitable tax credit and non-taxation of capital gains on gifts of publicly traded securities, ecologically sensitive land, and gifts of cultural property was almost $2.7 billion (Department of Finance, 2008). In policy terms, this cost is referred to as "tax expenditure" because it is functionally equivalent to direct government expenditure. Tax expenditures are a policy instrument that subsidizes the charitable sector by, in effect, approximately matching private donations. As a result, the charitable tax credit gives the appearance of a shrinking government, to the extent that tax expenditures reduce the direct expenditure budget.

Moral discourse about eliciting generosity as a national virtue has been applied to arguments for reducing social spending, but not to arguments for limiting tax incentives. In other words, neoliberal discourse represents the state as overly generous when it comes to providing social services, but not generous enough—to donors—when it comes to implementing the tax credit (Brooks, 2001). Ultimately, neoliberal restructuring, through the combination of cutting back direct funding and expanding tax incentives for philanthropy has made the nonprofit sector more, not less integrated with government, but also more competitive for both government contracts and private donations, and more dependent on and responsive to its benefactors.

The cultural redefinition of generosity from public to private facilitated these changes and signified a neoliberal watershed in political culture. Canadian fundraisers, attuned to these clashing views of national generosity, and seeking to emulate their American counterparts' fundraising success, worried that Canadians' expectations about the state's welfare role inhibited charitable donations. As Samantha put it:

> I don't think that Canada by any fault of its own is behind, I think it's the nature of the two different countries, of Canada up until relatively recently and the continuum of Canada's history has always been reliant on government. America has always been built from a premise of look after number one, the government ain't going to bail you out. (Samantha)

American trends persuaded fundraisers to associate less government with more giving. Although comparative and historical evidence contradicts the thesis that government spending "crowds out" philanthropy, the argument has a self-fulfilling quality. Concerns about "crowding out" became another rationale for government retrenchment, which Canadian fundraisers reinforced.

Notes

1. In contrast to the nonprofit sector, the criminal justice system was not subject to cutbacks in the 1990s. Public expenditure on the criminal justice system in Canada, including federal and provincial policing, courts, carceral institutions, and parole, increased throughout the 2000s, demonstrating that neoliberalism is more than merely a set of policies to reduce the size of government. An analysis of public accounts from 2002 to 2012 showed that per capita spending on the criminal justice system grew by 23% (in constant 2002 dollars) (Story & Yalkin, 2013). This per capita measure accounts for changes in the population size over these 11 years. In the same period, incidence of crime per capita decreased by the same amount, 23% (Story & Yalkin, 2013).

2. By 2019, wealth concentration in the top 1% of households had grown by 13% in Canada (to a 17.5% share) and by 8% in the U.S. (40.5% share). The top 10% also increased its share of wealth to 50.3% (Canada) and 76.6% (U.S.), which was an increase of 2% and 3%, respectively (OECD.stat, 2021).
3. The International Classification of Nonprofit Organizations (ICNO) uses 12 categories to describe nonprofit sectors, as follows: culture and recreation; education and research; health; social services; environment; development and housing; law, advocacy, and politics; philanthropic intermediaries and voluntarism promotion; international; religion; business and professional associations and unions; and others not elsewhere classified. Universities, colleges, and hospitals are often disaggregated from the education and health groups because the relatively small numbers of these institutions, their large operating budgets, and predominantly paid staff distinguish them from much of the nonprofit sector. For example, universities, colleges, and hospitals account for one-third of the paid workforce of Canada's entire nonprofit sector (Hall et al., 2005).
4. By 2020, government transfers remained the largest source of revenue for the nonprofit sector at over 55% of total income. Sales and fees accounted for 32%. Donations from households contributed less than 8%, while investments and corporate philanthropy were the smallest sources of income at 2.6% and 2.4%, respectively (Statistics Canada, 2022).

References

Adams, M. (2009). *Fire and Ice: United States, Canada and the Myth of Converging Values*. Penguin Canada.

Brooks, N. (2001). The Role of the Voluntary Sector in a Modern Welfare State. In J. Phillips, B. Chapman, & D. Stevens (Eds.), *Between State and Market: Essays on Charities Law and Policy in Canada* (pp. 166–216). McGill-Queen's University Press.

Clemens, J., & Samida, D. (1999). 1999 Private Charitable Generosity Index [Electronic Version]. *Public Policy Sources*, 13–18. http://www.fraserinstitute.org/researchandpublications/publications/2538.aspx

Cornelissen, L. (2021). Religiosity in Canada and Its Evolution from 1985 to 2019. Statistics Canada. https://www150.statcan.gc.ca/n1/en/pub/75-006-x/2021001/article/00010-eng.pdf?st=Lc7_k-7M

Department of Finance. (2008). *Tax Expenditures and Evaluations*. http://www.fin.gc.ca/taxexp-depfisc/2008/Taxexp-depfisc08_eng.pdf

Evans, B., Richmond, T., & Shields, J. (2005). Structuring Neoliberal Governance: The Nonprofit Sector, Emerging New Modes of Control and the Marketisation of Service Delivery. *Policy and Society, 24*(1), 73–97.

Fong, W. J. (2008). *J.W. McConnell: Financier, Philanthropist, Patriot.* McGill-Queen's University Press.

Gainer, A., Lammam, C., & Veldhuis, N. (2008). Generosity in Canada and the United States: The 2008 Generosity Index [Electronic Version]. *Fraser Alert.* http://www.fraserinstitute.org/commerce.web/product_files/Generosity_Index_2008.pdf

Hall, M. H., & Reed, P. B. (1998). Shifting the Burden: How Much Can Government Download to the Non-Profit Sector. *Canadian Public Administration / Administration Publique du Canada, 41*(1), 1–20.

Hall, M. H., Barr, C. W., Easwaramoorthy, M., Sokolowski, S. W., & Salamon, L. M. (2005). *The Canadian Nonprofit and Voluntary Sector in Comparative Perspective.* http://sectorsource.ca/sites/default/files/resources/files/jhu_report_en.pdf

Hall, M., Lasby, D., Ayer, S., & Gibbons, W. D. (2009). *Caring Canadians, Involved Canadians: Highlights from the 2007 National Survey of Giving, Volunteering and Participating.* Statistics Canada. https://publications.gc.ca/collections/collection_2009/statcan/71-542-X/71-542-x2009001-eng.pdf

Jackman, H. N. R. (1997). Private Giving in Canada. In J. Hannaford & E. P. Badovinac (Eds.), *The Empire Club of Canada Speeches 1996–1997* (pp. 534–545). The Empire Club Foundation.

Lasby, D., & Barr, C. (2018). *30 Years of Giving in Canada: The Giving Behaviour of Canadians: Who Gives, How, and Why?* Rideau Hall Foundation and Imagine Canada. https://imaginecanada.ca/sites/default/files/2019-05/30years_report_en.pdf

LeRoy, S., Veldhuis, N., & Clemens, J. (2002). The 2002 Generosity Index: Comparing Charitable Giving in Canada and the United States [Electronic Version]. *Fraser Forum,* 13–18. http://www.envision.ca/pdf/news/FraserInstitute.pdf

OECD.stat. (2021). Wealth Distribution by Country. Last Updated, December 2021. https://stats.oecd.org/index.aspx?queryid=81611

Pew Research Center. (2019). In U.S., Decline of Christianity Continues at Rapid Pace. https://www.pewresearch.org/religion/2019/10/17/in-u-s-decline-of-christianity-continues-at-rapid-pace/

Proceedings of the Standing Senate Committee on Banking, Trade and Commerce: Issues Dealing with Charitable Giving in Canada. (2004). First Session, 38th Parliament, Issue No. 4, Third, Fourth and Fifth Meetings Sess. (2004).

Reed, P. (2001, Autumn). Generosity: 30 Years of Giving. *Canadian Social Trends,* 11–13.

Stanford, J. (1998). The Rise and Fall of Deficit-mania: Public-Sector Finances and the Attack on Social Canada. In L. Samuelson & W. Antony (Eds.), *Power and Resistance: Critical Thinking about Canadian Social Issues* (2nd ed.). Fernwood Publishing.

Statistics Canada. (2022). *An Overview of the Non-profit Sector in Canada, 2010–2020.* Catalogue No. 13-605-X. https://www150.statcan.gc.ca/n1/en/pub/13-605-x/2022001/article/00002-eng.pdf?st=rIaLwf_j

Story, R., & Yalkin, T. R. (2013). *Expenditure Analysis of Criminal Justice in Canada.* Ottawa. https://publications.gc.ca/collections/collection_2013/dpb-pbo/YN5-49-2013-eng.pdf

Tillotson, S. (2008). *Contributing Citizens: Modern Charitable Fundraising and the Making of the Welfare State, 1920–66.* UBC Press.

Turcotte, M. (2015). Charitable Giving by Individuals. Spotlight on Canadians: Results from the General Social Survey. Statistics Canada. http://www.statcan.gc.ca/pub/89-652-x/89-652-x2015008-eng.pdf

Wooster, M. M. (2009). The Quiet Canadian. *Philanthropy Magazine* (Summer). http://www.philanthropyroundtable.org/topic/excellence_in_philanthropy/the_quiet_canadian

CHAPTER 6

"I Have to be Optimistic": Professional Fundraising and the Politics of Hope

Abstract This chapter reflects on the concept of hope as it was constructed through neoliberalism and deployed by the first large cohort of Canadian fundraisers. Beyond the fact that fundraising was a burgeoning career path in the early twenty-first century, fundraising was a "business of hope" in two other senses. First, fundraisers were identified as salespeople, selling the value and virtue of philanthropy for a better future. Second, fundraisers' optimism was a mode of governance, making philanthropic culture appear desirable as well as inevitable. Fundraisers advised donors to invest hope in the marketplace of charitable institutions even if steeper inequality and eroded democratic institutions followed from the unrelenting, unequal competition in that sector and throughout society.

Keywords Social imaginary • Optimism • Privatized hope • Neoliberal governance

Gail's fundraising career began with her layoff from a public relations position with a big corporation. While living on her severance pay, she started volunteering, lending her skills in event planning for a small, local health charity. Having studied business management with a focus on marketing and PR, she had never considered nonprofit work. When her volunteering led to a job offer, she joined the one other fundraiser in the office. Within

M.-B. Raddon, *The Business of Hope*, Palgrave Studies in Third Sector Research, https://doi.org/10.1007/978-3-031-18837-4_6

a few months, she was offered the senior position and began to introduce a suite of fundraising methods that she learned on the job.

I spoke with Gail 20 years after this first fundraising job, when she was 4 years into the role of Director of Major Gifts for the provincial office of a national health charity, her fifth fundraising position. I asked about her outlook on Canadian fundraising as someone who had witnessed long-term trends. Her response exemplified the optimism that many fundraisers considered part of their role:

> As fundraisers, we work with philanthropists, and I think part of our outlook, and who we are as people is, we're always so very positive and always thinking that there's opportunity. And that's how we look at what we do in life generally. [...] We always see opportunity, that's what our job is! (laughing). (Gail)

The timing of my interviews corresponded with the "great recession" of 2008–2009. Endowed funds were plummeting in value and donors were backing out of long-term commitments. Even so, Canada's leading fundraisers presented a perennially positive outlook. For example, when Sherry, the senior associate of a national consulting firm, spoke about her recently missed targets, she added, "I have to be optimistic, I'm a fundraiser." Gail also acknowledged the recession in passing: "Even when people talk about, you know, 'We could be going into recession, this could be a very bad time,' but people [fundraisers] always say, there's always this other opportunity. So, I always have a positive outlook."

Gail and Sherry would not allow an economic recession to cloud the neoliberal social imaginary they projected—their shared vision of the state of society and of the future—characterized by pervasive optimism. Their counterpart, Todd, was introduced in the first chapter as a relatively young fundraiser who had catapulted from being a university call centre manager to the top executive of a large health charity. He dubbed the occupation, "the business of hope," epitomizing this social imaginary.

The "business of hope" can be interpreted as operating in two ways: as a literal expression of fundraisers' sales work to solicit donations and major gifts, and as a metaphor for neoliberal governance that made the marketization of social life (e.g., voting with our dollars) seem the right way to divine and determine the public good.

Fundraising as a "business of hope" communicated more than fundraisers' enthusiasm for their own work and careers, although they had reason to be enthusiastic about their personal opportunities. Fundraising as an occupation in this period offered entrants excellent prospects. Fundraisers were in high demand, with 60% of survey respondents in 2002 reporting that their organization had increased the number of paid staff during that year alone (Saunders, 2003). In the same survey of 1393 Canadian fundraisers, 78% said their current work was "satisfying" or "very satisfying," with workload said to be the largest downside, followed by pay (Saunders, 2003).[1]

Dissatisfaction about pay may be attributed to the wide range of salaries across different sizes and types of agencies, a persistent gender pay gap across all salary levels, and the growing number of entrants from backgrounds in private sector occupations with comparatively higher pay scales. Nevertheless, the demand for fundraisers was quickly pushing up salaries. At the time of my interviews (2009), the median income of all Canadian fundraisers was $70,000, and the top 25% earned at least $93,000 annually. For fundraisers with 10 years' experience, the median annual income was $77,500, and the top 25% earned over $100,000 (Healey et al., 2010). By comparison, the median annual *family* income for all Canadians in that year, 2009, was $48,900 (in constant 2011 dollars) (Statistics Canada, 2015).

For these reasons, it is easy to see why successful fundraisers of this cohort would feel positively about their own career prospects and about the whole industry. For example, Joyce, the president of a hospital foundation, whose 18-year career had covered many areas of fundraising, layered optimism about the future of fundraising onto a neoliberal forecast:

> I think we're developing a culture of philanthropy. [...] I think more people are getting aware of what the opportunities are, and also the fact that the government is not going to do it all, and they can't do it all. So, I think the future is pretty promising for us. (Joyce)

The bright side of the loss of confidence in the social role of governments, for Joyce, was the opportunity for a cultural shift towards reliance on philanthropy. The undermining of the welfare state exposed charitable organizations to social need, which boded well for the future of fundraising. However, fundraisers' optimism was not limited to their profession alone; they were generally optimistic about the efficacy of their work as fundraisers. In the introduction to a collection of essays on philanthrocapitalism, Gavin Fridell and Martijn Konings (2013) interpret such optimism as a feature of neoliberalism. They noted: "despite mounting evidence of a strong connection between neoliberal economic policies and growing inequality, … there remains a widely held sense of optimism in the West … about neoliberalism's ability to eliminate the very problems it helps to create" (p. 7).

Fundraising as Privatized Hope

Many fundraisers saw their work as a kind of sales business. For instance, Anne, a fundraiser of 19 years for two universities, a hospital, and a provincial arts organization, defended the business orientation of her occupation, saying: "I don't care what anybody says, we're salespeople and I don't think that's a bad thing." As salespeople, fundraisers crafted a pitch, tailored it to specific prospects, and used a wide range of sales techniques to secure donations, according to their branch of fundraising and organizational strategy: annual, monthly, or legacy giving, special events, online giving, major gifts, and so on (Mallabone, 2022). Sales often succeeded when fundraisers could tap into donors' hopes that they could make a positive difference by putting money where it was needed. Following the gift agreement, fundraisers worked in a stewarding role, continuing to affirm donors' hopes that their generosity would result in improved lives (Moreau, 2022).

What did it mean, sociologically, that charitable institutions were selling hope in this period of neoliberalism? For Ronald Aronson (2017), neoliberalization entails the "privatization of hope," which he defines as the "maddening profusion of personal hopes," amidst an assault on, "the kind of hope that is social, the motivation behind movements to make the world freer, more equal, more democratic, and more livable" (p. 116). Private hope refers to hope for one's own life and family, such as winning the lottery, getting a better job, or curbing an addiction. As neoliberalism has come to incorporate an element of community responsibility, privatized hope also refers to hope for healthier communities through the uncoordinated, private action of individuals, through volunteering and donating.

Fundraisers privatized hope by promising individuals that their chosen charitable or philanthropic activity would make a difference. In doing so, they put social hope—shared hope in, and born of, social action—outside the frame. Wendy Brown writes:

> The neoliberal solution to problems is always more markets, more complete markets, more perfect markets, more financialization, new technologies, new ways to monetize. Anything but collaborative and contestatory human decision making, control over the conditions of existence, planning for the future; anything but deliberate constructions of existence through democratic discussion, law, policy. Anything but the human knowledge, deliberation, judgment, and action classically associated with *homo politicus*. (Brown, 2015, pp. 221–2)

Privatizing hope in fundraising was another way to extend market rationality in response to the social need that neoliberal policies themselves generated, further shifting *homo politicus* towards *homo oeconomicus* as neoliberalism's preferred default rationality.

Brown argues that privatized hope is actually reflective of civilizational despair. She is not suggesting that civilizational despair is uniquely a neoliberal phenomenon. However, she argues that neoliberal rationality, "[through] its figuration of the human, its reality principle, and its worldview—'there is no alternative'—consecrates, deepens, and naturalizes without acknowledging this despair" (2015, p. 221).

Fundraisers in the late 2000s had evidence to contradict their optimism and spark concern, even before the global financial crisis. There were signs that the culture of philanthropy they were attempting to foster was a plutocratic culture and that efforts to make charitable giving widespread in the population were failing. Years later, we can see that the extraordinary fundraising trends of 1995 through the end of 2007 set this period apart and have not been matched since (Lasby & Barr, 2018). As reported by the Canada Revenue Agency through tax-receipted donations, from 1985 to 1990, charitable revenues grew rapidly at 4.4% per year, and then levelled off over the next five years from 1990 to 1995. Starting in 1995, revenues surged at an average annual increase of 5.6% until 2007. Each year saw record-breaking totals until Canadian charitable revenues had almost doubled from $5 billion in 2005 to $9.6 billion just prior to the financial crisis (Lasby & Barr, 2018).

Significantly, in the same period, the number of Canadians who made charitable donations shrank despite population growth. In the 12-year zenith of fundraising (1995–2007), the growth in revenues came from major philanthropy. This growth trend proved to be unsustainable. Since the recession of 2008 and 2009, the lion's share of fundraising revenue has continued to come from top donors, but totals have fluctuated below the peak in 2007. Since 2008, individual donations per capita have also continued to trend downward (Lasby & Barr, 2018).

The next major economic shock, the COVID-19 pandemic, further confounded the hope that individuals could and would step up with donations in a time of social need. In November 2020, Imagine Canada surveyed 1000 charitable organizations with annual revenues above $30,000 (excluding religious congregations) on the pandemic's impact on their revenue, demand, and capacity. The survey found that a third of organizations, primarily in education, health, social services, and other human services, experienced a combination of increased demand and diminished capacity to deliver services. For many organizations, the loss of capacity was due, in part, to diminished revenues from gifts and donations. Three-quarters of organizations found they raised less money through at least one form of fundraising, primarily events-based fundraising, as expected, but over a third of charities reported that they had also lost revenue from a downturn in major gifts (Lasby, 2021).

Despite awareness of disturbing trends and dire social needs, fundraisers' professional organizations often push attitudes of hopefulness. A quick keyword search for "hope" on the Hilborn Charity eNews blog, a go-to source of news and analysis for Canadian fundraisers, yields 200 hits, with many of the blog posts including "hope" in the title.[2] These discourses of hope reinforce Barbara Ehrenreich's (2009) arguments about the widespread optimism in American business culture, in which "positive thinking has made itself useful as an apology for the crueler aspects of the market economy" (p. 8). Such optimism, says Ehrenreich, closes off avenues of critical thinking and papers over more complex emotions that support the capacity for political analysis and social action (see also Scharff, 2016).

As an expert occupation with proximity to business elites, fundraisers are not alone in cleaving to privatized hope. Raewyn Connell's (2010) study of Australian managers in the knowledge economy explored the "interplay of neoliberal capitalism and intellectual production." Connell interviewed 12 managers about their intellectual labour, such as strategic planning. These interviews focused on the topic of the social surplus, defined as "the available material resources of society" (p. 779). In all but two cases, Connell's managers embraced the neoliberal consensus and spoke as allies of corporate power. Yet, Connell observed that the pressure-filled conditions of their work life, such as busyness and stress, did not permit reflection. More complex and oppositional ways of thinking were unlikely for this group because "the possibility of *reflective* intellectual work [was] constantly undermined by the conditions of managerial labor" (p. 789).

Likewise, fundraisers' positive thinking could be understood as stemming from the particular expectations of their work as fundraisers. Required to make a "case for support" that was confident and compelling, they could scarcely afford to perform critique or acknowledge despair. Yet without distress and outrage, without the impetus and intellectual wherewithal to conceive political alternatives, engage with political conflict, and fashion political action, the "business of hope" cannot deliver social hope.

Fundraisers should not be held responsible for rectifying the devastating effects of under-funding, privatization, and macro-economic conditions. Though fundraisers do good work on their own terms, they cannot be expected to disrupt neoliberal rationality without support and resources from beyond their own professional circles. Critical analysis necessary for social hope may be found in the work of groups such as Incite! Women of Color Against Violence, a radical editorial collective that penned a series of critical essays on the "non-profit industrial complex" (Incite! 2007). Their book title, *The Revolution will not be Funded: Beyond the Nonprofit Industrial Complex*, updates and pays homage to Gil Scott Heron's 1971 lyric, "the revolution will not be televised." In this spirit, they challenge nonprofit workers to learn from grassroots, democratic, progressive movements about nonprofits' political limitations, and alternative formations.

Fundraising and Neoliberal Governance

Long pre-dating neoliberalism, in the gilded age of the nineteenth-century United States, the standard critique of large-scale philanthropy was that the robber barons' largess served to legitimate their oligarchic power, exploitation, and massive wealth accumulation (Wagner, 2000). This standard critique is seldom heard in relation to twenty-first-century major donors (but see Callahan, 2017). A new element that distinguishes the previous era of extreme inequality from neoliberal capitalism is neoliberal governance. It is contemporary forms of governance that account for this dulling of class-based critique and class conflict.

Neoliberal governance refers to a soft, horizontal mode of power that augments the direct, coercive rule of the state and gives corporate and financial capital a friendly face. Brown (2015) describes the relationship of neoliberalism and governance in this way:

> Governance has become neoliberalism's primary administrative form, the political modality through which it creates environments, structures constraints and incentives, and hence conducts subjects. Contemporary neoliberalism is unthinkable without governance. (p. 122)

The neoliberal state layers governance onto existing institutional ways of exercising power and authority coercively such as law, policing, collective bargaining, and overtly political processes involving contestation, class conflict, partisanship, brokering, and opposition. By contrast to institutional power, governance is a more diffuse, dispersed, and decentred form of rule, which is conducted, for instance, through agencies of the nonprofit and voluntary sector. Governance operates through management and administration, partnerships and networking, dialogue, and deliberation. Governance sidelines politics, in the sense of power struggles, conflict, and negotiation. Given its participatory form, governance makes power difficult to name and oppose, which undermines political contestation over different visions of justice and the public good.

In this way, neoliberal governance depoliticizes social struggles by making political power, including class power, less visible. Governance brings people on board neoliberal economic rationality and fosters the impression that we are all working towards a common goal. The social imaginary of optimism and the privatization of hope are primary tools of governance. Social hope, in contrast, feeds on political action, just as social movement mobilization requires social hope as its impetus.

A governance analysis of fundraising offers insight into how neoliberalism takes hold in everyday life at a distance from elite circles of corporate and financial power. The neoliberal rationality that infuses fundraising and many social fields is not imposed but nevertheless enjoys a broad cultural consensus. In Brown's words:

> Modern political power is extraordinary in its range and reach precisely because it is so relentlessly intermixed with daily life, so intimate with us

> where we are most needy and vulnerable, so without scruple in producing and incorporating these needs as part of its own expansion. (Brown, 2007, p. 11)

Fundraising is a quintessential case of Brown's analysis of neoliberalism's expansion through social vulnerability. Vulnerability is created in the first place as governments devolve responsibility for an array of social and community services to nonprofit and voluntary organizations without sufficient funds for core functions. In this governance arrangement, as Brown (2015) argues, "large-scale problems, such as recessions, finance-capital crises, unemployment, or environmental problems, as well as fiscal crises of the state, are sent down the pipeline to small and weak units unable to cope with them technically, politically or financially" (p. 132).

This devolution of social responsibility has brought forth fundraisers' best entrepreneurial efforts and entrenched the "business of hope" in Canada's political economy. This devolution of responsibility explains how a middle and working-class occupational group with high ideals for social betterment across a wide range of causes took on neoliberal goals such as expanding government tax expenditures to cultivate large philanthropy. It explains why fundraisers as a group endorsed market solutions, why they celebrated extremes of wealth, why they discredited government service delivery, and why they sought opportunities to enhance elites' hyper-agency in advancing philanthrocapitalist projects.

Like other professionals, fundraisers lack opportunity for introspection, and their culture of positivity leaves little room for critical examination. By and large, they believe they do good work that is above politics, but their depoliticized practices offer only privatized hope. For Michael Apple, demobilization due to loss of social hope is, "a disaster in a time of radical reconstruction of education, health care, social services, and the entire public sector" (Apple, 2012, p. 148). To revitalize hope and counter cynicism, the nonprofit sector needs to be re-politicized. We especially need to reframe social change as a collective goal in an inequitable society, not as the automatic result of individuals' personal choices in a market of charities.

Apple (2012), citing social theorist, Raymond Williams, argues that social hope is a vital resource in times of crisis. He reminds us of victories won in the political struggles of social movements within longstanding political traditions. Oppositional movements for socially just institutional arrangements need to be restored to collective memory as viable alternatives. All too often, neoliberal ideologies suggest that previous social movements were failed projects rather than models of change from which we may continue to draw lessons to develop educated hope:

> The fact that there is such a long history of successful progressive movements in so many sectors in all of our countries provides a necessary resource when we are constantly being told that the neoliberal agenda is the only solution to the crisis that it itself created. (Apple, 2012, p. 148)

From this perspective, social hope—as educated hope and as historical memory—is not merely a rosy outlook.

How can such hope arise in bleak times? Some say social hope, like holding a light in the darkness, "constitutes its own conditions" (Thompson, 2013, p. 7). We only need to look for it. Others say the flame must be fanned and hope must be learned (Apple, 2012). Either way, as a society, we need shared hope to envision and collectively work in new directions. Nonprofits and fundraisers need to work together, with and within progressive social movements, to facilitate the political awareness and policy changes needed to challenge the business of hope that neoliberal capitalism generates. Social hope declares that by funding social and cultural needs sufficiently, fairly, and transparently, and through democratic, political allocation processes, we lay the foundations for a better world.

Notes

1. Survey results on job satisfaction differed significantly by gender. Eighty-three percent of men were satisfied with the job in general compared to 76% of women. When asked about specific aspects of the job, such as pay, workload, training opportunities, and career advancement, women's satisfaction was 9–12 percentage points below men's (Saunders, 2003). These differences make sense in view of the gender gap in compensation at all levels of the profession and the disproportionate number of men who occupied the high-status roles (Healey et al., 2010). Women, who made up 85% of the non-managerial fundraising workforce, earned on average only 79% of what men earned (Healey et al., 2010).
2. See https://hilborn-charityenews.ca.

References

Apple, M. W. (2012). Afterword on Neoliberalism, the Current Crisis, and The Politics of Hope. In M. Lall (Ed.), *Policy, Discourse and Rhetoric: How New Labour Challenged Social Justice and Democracy* (pp. 141–150). Sense Publishers.

Aronson, R. (2017). *We: Reviving Social Hope*. University of Chicago Press.

Brown, W. (2007). Democracy and Bad Dreams. *Theory & Event, 10*(1). https://doi.org/10.1353/tae.2007.0036

Brown, W. (2015). *Undoing the Demos: Neoliberalism's Stealth Revolution*. Zone Books.

Callahan, D. (2017). *The Givers: Wealth, Power and Philanthropy in a New Gilded Age*. Vintage Books.

Connell, R. (2010). Building the Neoliberal World: Managers as Intellectuals in a Peripheral Economy. *Critical Sociology, 36*(6), 777–792.

Ehrenreich, B. (2009). *Bright-Sided: How the Relentless Promotion of Positive Thinking Is Undermining America*. Metropolitan Books.

Fridell, G., & Konings, M. (Eds.). (2013). *Age of Icons: Exploring Philanthrocapitalism in the Contemporary World*. University of Toronto Press.

Healey, R., Bartolini, B., Maehara, P. V., & Williams, C. (2010). *2009–2010 AFP Compensation and Benefits Study*. Association of Fundraising Professionals.

Incite! Women of Color Against Violence (Ed.). (2007). *The Revolution Will Not be Funded: Beyond the Non-profit Industrial Complex*. South End Press.

Lasby, D. (2021, February). *Imagine Canada's Sector Monitor: Ongoing Effects of the COVID-19 Pandemic*. Imagine Canada. https://imaginecanada.ca/en/360/ongoing-impacts-covid-19-crisis-charitable-sector

Lasby, D., & Barr, C. (2018). *30 Years of Giving in Canada: The Giving Behaviour of Canadians: Who Gives, How, and Why?* Rideau Hall Foundation and Imagine Canada. https://imaginecanada.ca/sites/default/files/2019-05/30years_report_en.pdf

Mallabone, G. (Ed.). (2022). *Excellence in Fundraising in Canada: The Definitive Resource for Canadian Fundraisers* (Vol. 1, 2nd ed.). Civil-Sector Press.

Moreau, L. (2022). Stewardship. In G. Mallabone (Ed.), *Excellence in Fundraising in Canada: The Definitive Resource for Canadian Fundraisers* (Vol. 1, 2nd ed., pp. 297–310). Civil-Sector Press.

Saunders, R. (2003). *AFP/CPRN Survey of Fundraisers*. Paper presented at the Presentation at AFP International Conference on Fundraising, Toronto. http://www.cprn.org/documents/18631_en.pdf

Scharff, C. (2016). The Psychic Life of Neoliberalism: Mapping the Contours of Entrepreneurial Subjectivity. *Theory, Culture and Society, 33*(6), 107–122.

Statistics Canada. (2015). Average and Median Total Income by Census Family Type, Table 11-10-0162-01. https://doi.org/10.25318/1110016201-eng. https://www150.statcan.gc.ca/t1/tbl1/en/tv.action?pid=1110016201

Thompson, P. (2013). The Privatization of Hope and the Crisis of Negation. In P. Thompson & S. Žižek (Eds.), *The Privatization of Hope: Ernst Bloch and the Future of Utopia* (pp. 1–20). Duke University Press.

Wagner, D. (2000). *What's Love Got to Do with It: A Critical Look at American Charity*. New Press.

Appendix: Research Methods

Selection of Participants

This study draws on a set of in-depth, qualitative interviews I conducted in 2008 and 2009 with seasoned fundraisers from across Canada. I chose research participants who had at least a decade of experience, a senior position within their organization, and a strong identification with fundraising as a career, as demonstrated through a combination of professional service, publications, teaching appointments in fundraising programmes, and fundraising credentials. To identify individuals who met these criteria, I combed the online listings of the executive office holders of local chapters of professional organizations such as the Association of Fundraising Professionals, Canadian Association of Gift Planners, Canadian Council for the Advancement of Education, or Association for Healthcare Philanthropy. I also looked up lists of past speakers at professional conferences whose career biographies were publicized. I then reviewed the lists to see if they included a wide range of nonprofit organizations. If some sectors were missing, I searched organizations' websites to identify senior fundraising staff, checked their career biographies on the professional networking site LinkedIn, and added more names.

After compiling several names for each city or region, I numbered the lists to make a sampling frame and used a random number generator to select a sample of names from each list. The constraints of time and

M.-B. Raddon, *The Business of Hope*, Palgrave Studies in Third Sector Research, https://doi.org/10.1007/978-3-031-18837-4

distance limited the number of interviews I could complete to 50 in total: Vancouver (10), Montreal (4), Halifax (6), Toronto (20), Ottawa (5), and 1 each in the southern Ontario cities of Kingston, Ajax, Burlington, Hamilton, and London. I contacted the members of my sample through published workplace email addresses. All but two agreed to my interview request and I selected two replacements from my lists. Those I interviewed often suggested names of other senior fundraisers and offered to make introductions. Although I declined this "snowball method" of selection to protect participants' confidentiality, many of the referrals were already listed in my sampling frame, which affirmed that my method of compiling names based on fundraisers' online presence had succeeded in identifying leaders of the profession by reputation.

The ratio of 32 women to 18 men in my sample (64% female) over-represented men in the Canadian fundraising industry, which was 75% female. But, as expected, my sample better reflected the gender ratio of fundraisers in senior ranks where mens' presence is disproportionate to their numbers in the profession as a whole (Healey et al., 2010). Even within my sample 50 of experienced fundraisers, gender stratification at the top of the profession was evident, with the 18 men unequally distributed within the highest ranked positions. In terms of racial identities, my sample reflected the profession, which in 2009 was 90% white (Healey et al., 2010).

Each of the 50 fundraisers had at least 10 years' experience except one who, in the ninth year of her career, had started her third job as a fundraising executive for a business school at a large university. On average, the fundraisers had over 18 years' experience. Half had worked as fundraisers for over 19 years at the time of the interview. The longest career was 34 years.

Thirty-six of the 50 had earned the professional designation, Certified Fund-Raising Executive (CFRE), including 2 who had also attained a higher honorific. Thirteen had fundraising education and credentials from a university or college programme, many in addition to the CFRE, and most of these had also taught fundraising as part-time university or college instructors.

As mentioned, the 50 fundraisers worked in 5 of Canada's major cities. As their seniority would predict, they tended to be employed in large organizations. None worked in the same organization. The largest number (14) worked for consulting firms that served a wide range of clients, from large organizations running multimillion-dollar capital campaigns to small charities that did not have a fundraising staff. Half of these consultants were principals of their own businesses and the others held senior positions in national or international firms. The next largest group represented hospital foundations (10), followed by universities or research institutes (7), disease-specific health charities (6), arts or cultural organizations (3), and charities addressing issues of poverty (3), international development and humanitarian work (2), and environmental concerns (1). One participant headed the fundraising activities of a prestigious independent school, another directed the fundraising body of a religious organization, another led a community foundation, and another held the top job at a national organization whose mission prominently involved promoting philanthropy.

The fundraisers' job titles varied. Among the 50, there were 30 different designations, with titles and rank related to the size and type of a fundraising shop. Approximately a third of participants occupied the highest position in the organization, sometimes with a partner (with titles such as President, Executive Director, or Principal), another third headed departments or offices responsible for fundraising within larger organizations (such as Director of Philanthropy), and the remaining third held more specialized offices (with titles such as Director of Planned Giving). The one participant who was unemployed at the time of the interview was hired within a few weeks as the fundraising director of the Canadian branch of an international humanitarian organization.

The fundraisers' educational backgrounds and prior work history were varied. Participants were highly educated as a group, almost all with at least a university degree. Liberal arts degrees were as common as business degrees, followed by professional degrees (in fields such as social work, education, journalism, teaching, and law), and these only slightly exceeded the number of science degrees. Almost half had post-graduate degrees, most commonly a Master of Business Administration (7). Their professions prior to entering fundraising reflected the diversity of their educational backgrounds. The sample was roughly divided between those with business backgrounds (advertising, management, marketing, sales, public relations, financial planning) and those who had started their careers in an array of other fields in the social services, arts, or technology.

Only four participants had been with the same organization for the duration of their fundraising career, and these were large organizations that allowed them to gain specializations as they rose in the ranks. Over half of the fundraisers had worked in three or more organizations prior to their current position. Collectively, participants had worked for 283 different organizations, not including the consultants, who had served hundreds of institutional clients. In addition to movement between organizations, several members of the group had made geographical moves during their careers. Although I was not able to interview in the Prairie Provinces or northern Canada, my participants as a group had lived and worked as fundraisers in all regions of English-speaking Canada. Some had also worked in the United States and elsewhere abroad.

I did not ask participants explicitly about their political affiliations, but five mentioned that their prior careers had included fundraising or campaigning for a national or provincial political party. These five represented parties on the left, right, and centre of the political spectrum. A few others expressly stated their political leanings in the interview, which confirmed that the sample included a mix of political affiliations.

The Interviews

I conducted 45 of the interviews in person and 5 by telephone. Interviews were usually 60–90 minutes in duration and took place where the participant chose, including their workplaces, local eateries, and occasionally their own homes. My interview practices accorded with common qualitative research methods for semi-structured, ethnographic interviews (Hesse-Biber, 2017; Roulston, 2010). The interviews were conversational, guided by a list of open-ended questions, and designed to elicit description of fundraisers' "cultural worlds" (Roulston, 2010, p. 19). I started by inviting participants to recount how their career in fundraising began and how they had arrived at their present position. I also asked about the importance they placed on attaining fundraising credentials such as the CFRE designation and participating in professional membership organizations such as the Association of Fundraising Professionals.

Early in the interview I asked everyone, "What is the most significant change in fundraising you have observed over the course of your career?" After discussing initial responses, I invited participants to reflect on their experiences related to a set of topics that trade publications had identified as philanthropic trends (Hilborn Civil Sector Press, n.d.; KCI Philanthropy, n.d.). These included but were not limited to the growth of fundraising for major gifts, the professionalization of the occupation, donors' changing relationship to nonprofits, expansion of the tax incentives for charitable donations, nonprofits' reliance on professional fundraising, and the impact of the economic recession on fundraising. I also asked about the qualities and attributes that make for a good fundraiser and the satisfactions of fundraising as work. I showed equal interest in the converse: talk of poor fundraisers, failure, and work dissatisfaction, but fundraisers' culture of positivity somewhat held these topics in check. I guided the interviews so that most participants commented on each topic, but I also allowed them to direct the conversation according to the relevance of each topic to their own work. This flexible approach allowed for new topics to emerge, such as comparisons with the United States, which informed my analysis as much as the responses to my prepared questions.

The digitally recorded interviews were transcribed verbatim in a standard orthographic format that basically described the conversation without attempting to represent the speech in exacting detail (Hammersley, 2010). All participants received an electronic copy of their transcript with an invitation to add, withdraw, or clarify any statements, not as an attempt to achieve veracity but to elicit further reflection. Only one person offered small amendments.

When writing about participants, I have masked their identities by referring to them by first name pseudonyms, omitting their cities, and slightly altering details about their position, sector, or biography. Pseudonyms were selected to loosely match the popularity of participants' actual names in the decade when they were born. In this way, pseudonyms reflect participants' generation, but otherwise have no relationship to their actual names.

Qualitative Discourse Analysis of Neoliberalism

The process of analysis of the interviews was theoretically guided by writings on neoliberalism as a governing political-economic rationality and by analytical approaches influenced by Michel Foucault: governmentality studies and critical discourse analysis. To get started, it was helpful to borrow techniques from grounded theory for sifting through the volume of textual data. The first tasks included re-reading the 785 single-spaced pages of transcripts as a body of work, drafting a synopsis of each interview, and creating tabular summaries of participants' details, which I completed with an undergraduate student research assistant, Meaghan Hiller. Using the method of "constant comparison," we generated a coding scheme to categorize and sort the interview content, including topics that were planned and those that came about unexpectedly (Glaser, 1965;

Hesse-Biber & Leavy, 2010). This process involved making short marginal notes to label content that arose repeatedly. By referring to previous notes and comparing recurring topics, we created a provisional set of 23 codes (similar to key word tags on blog posts) with brief explanatory definitions that could summarize most of the content of the interviews with some overlap. For example, all comments about the elimination of the capital gains tax on donations of publicly traded securities and any other remarks on the tax treatment of donations in Canada were coded as "tax incentives." When participants spoke about how Canada's tax incentives for charitable donations differed from tax incentives in the United States and elsewhere, we also applied the code "transnational comparison," resulting in text that was doubly coded.

Meaghan Hiller and I independently applied the coding scheme to several of the same interviews to check that we were interpreting the codes and text similarly. We discussed our discrepant interpretations and considered how to include topics that did not seem to be captured by the existing codes. Through this process, we refined the coding scheme by adding a few new codes or revising the working definition of others (Glaser & Strauss, 1967). We then used the computer-assisted qualitative data analysis program HyperRESEARCH to affix one or more codes to the meaningful segments of text throughout all the transcripts. Once the coding was complete, the computer program assisted analysis by generating lists of excerpted statements related to each code. The richest codes, and those most relevant to neoliberalism, became the broad topics of analytical interest for the chapters of this book.

Coding the interviews was preliminary to a discourse analysis, the main research method of the book. While there are many systems of discourse analysis of interviews, I took a post-structural approach. Basic to post-structuralism is the idea that discourses are not merely self-evident representations of social reality, but actively produce and constitute the social realities they describe. In Foucault's words, discourses are "practices that systematically form the objects of which they speak" (Foucault, 1972, p. 49; cited by Mills, 2004, p. 15). As Sara Mills (2004) explained, discursive structures, or the "building blocks" of discourse,

> can be detected because of the systematicity of the ideas, opinions, concepts, ways of thinking and behaving which are formed within a particular context, and because of the effects of those ways of thinking and behaving. Thus, we can assume that there is a set of discourses of femininity and masculinity, because women and men behave within a certain range of parameters when defining themselves as gendered subjects. (pp. 15–16)

To re-state Mills' definition for the present study, we can read discourses of neoliberalism in the context of the Canadian fundraising industry because of the effects of the "systematicity of the ideas, opinions, concepts, ways of thinking and behaving," regarding all the ways the social was being shaped along the model of free (and financialized) markets, including through economic policies of privatization, deregulation, and competitive bidding for contracts, as well as normalizing entrepreneurship, competitive self-enhancement, individualism, and personal responsibility.

Crucially, the effects of dominant discourses are to render some thoughts, speakers, and bodies sensible and reasonable, and others peculiar, out of place, off base, or unintelligible. In this way, neoliberal discourses accomplish and affirm the permeation of market rationality through all areas of life, so we come to identify market logic with common sense. Yet, the analysis of discourse needs to be more than a descriptive account of prevailing ideas and attitudes. Otherwise, dominant discourses such as neoliberalism would appear monolithic and research accounts such as this would lack explanatory power (Springer, 2016, p. 20). Post-structural analysis avoids conjuring neoliberalism as singular, all-powerful, and self-reproducing by treating discourses as sites of struggle over the construction of social reality, normality, and morality. In other words, discourses are not imposed on us through power exercised from above but are constituted through encounters with other discourses vying for status as truth in micro-processes of power (Brock et al., 2012; van Dijk, 1993). Foucault expressed these political struggles over the "truth" of discourse with the term "power/knowledge" to underscore that power operates by constituting fields of knowledge (Foucault, 1980). It follows that discourses are knowable in their contestation with other discourses, and we can observe how power works whenever competing discourses either mesh or clash (Mills, 2004, p. 136).

The practice of discourse analysis for this study, then, involved close analysis of the transcripts for their correspondence with wider discursive structures. For example, to examine neoliberalization in participants' talk of creating a "culture of philanthropy," I gathered the relevant pages of the transcripts and moved between immediate interpretive questions (What would a culture of philanthropy look like? What is its significance? What are its constitutive elements? What is its constitutive outside? How would it come about?), and broader questions of social analysis (How would a culture of philanthropy deepen or disrupt existing relations of power? How would it bring certain social realities into view and obscure others? What would it normalize? What moral evaluations would it carry?).

While asking such questions, I sought to bring the interviews into conversation with more abstract social theory. For example, Wendy Brown's (2015) theoretical analysis of rival conceptions of the human that animate modernity, *homo politicus* and *homo oeconomicus*, suggested a framework for understanding participants' political talk. Brown writes that the figure of *homo politicus* is "the most important casualty of the ascendance of neoliberal reason" (p. 87). *Homo politicus* refers to:

> the creature animated by and for the realization of popular sovereignty as well as its own individual sovereignty, ... the substance and legitimacy of whatever democracy might mean beyond securing the individual provisioning of individual ends; this 'beyond' includes political equality and freedom, representation, popular sovereignty, and deliberation and judgment about the public good and the common. (pp. 86–87)

Brown argues that *homo oeconomicus*, the defining figure of neoliberal rationality, has vanquished *homo politicus* and become normative across political, social, and economic spheres. *Homo oeconomicus* configures citizen-subjects as human capital, and state institutions as firms, all of which are driven to enhance their market value and competitive positioning even in spheres of life where markets have never existed. Brown's analysis offered insight into my participants' political discussion.

In every interview, I was interested in the discourses that participants mobilized in response to ethical and political questions. However, the way participants responded turned out to be as revealing as what they said. On questions of ethics, participants were animated. For example, the topic of donor-designated gifts arose in most interviews, and I would ask, what do fundraisers do when their prospective major donors targeted gifts in ways that would not actually fulfil institutional priorities? To this question, most fundraisers spoke as though on script. They insisted that professional ethics called for them to facilitate a dialogue between the donor and charity until both were satisfied with the terms of the gift. As I listened, I could make out a tension underlying their ardency because "donor-centric" fundraising, a common theme of the fundraising literature (Burk, 2003; Davis, 2015; Peacock, 2007), was a competing professional ideal. To the degree that donor-centrism conflicted with the requirement to avoid "mission-drift," that is, to serve organizations' fundraising needs and not be driven by dollar targets, fundraisers took pains to assert their ethical position on the side of organizations. Failing to do so would undermine the reputation of the profession. In the face of public scrutiny of the nonprofit sector, they were emphatic that their job is to facilitate agreements between donors and charities to convert ill-conceived or self-serving gifts into gifts that meet charities' identified needs.

On political topics, the interviews flowed differently. For example, when discussing tax incentives for philanthropy, fundraisers, by and large, seemed to have less to say, as though opinion on the topic was self-evident and simply beyond debate. With near unanimity, they approved of enlarging tax incentives. Their professional bodies had been lobbying for more favourable tax treatment of donations, especially the elimination of capital gains tax on gifts of appreciated publicly traded securities. Their incremental successes starting in the 1990s had accelerated major gift fundraising for large nonprofits (Duff, 2001). Fundraisers' opinion of tax incentives was shared among those with different political identities, those who worked outside the major gift specialty, and those who worked with small nonprofits that did not benefit from major gifts. The prevailing view aligned with neoliberal common sense of lower taxes and devolved government.

From the point of view of discourse analysis, what was interesting was how difficult it was for me, as the interviewer, to articulate contrary perspectives. I attempted to deepen the discussion by introducing critiques of the tax credit, characterizing it as a government subsidy of philanthropy, for example. Haltingly, I suggested that income tax credits, which can amount to over 50% of the value of major donations, represent foregone tax revenue, money that was donated instead of taxed. Tax-credited donations undemocratically channel funds away from public coffers and into organizations that donors alone choose. The tax credit, I suggested, represents "public money" that is allocated by wealthy individuals and escapes the public scrutiny and political deliberation of budgeted, direct spending.

No matter how much I rehearsed my questions about the political legitimacy of the tax credit, these questions came across awkwardly and I had difficulty making myself clear. I received tangential responses from those who seemed not to have understood what I was driving at, and polite rebuttals from others. A few admitted that they had never heard the tax credit debated among colleagues, at conferences, or as part of their training. One participant, who followed the argument, found the discursive clash funny and explained to me, through her laughter, why my line of questioning had failed:

> So, no, nobody ever in this profession talks about how a capital gains tax is a redistribution of wealth (chuckling). Like in other words, like, no (laughing). No, and it wouldn't even cross their minds that they should be concerned about something that benefits the wealthy [donor] because they're *good*. The wealthy are the good guys, especially if they're giving us money. (Vivian)

It was in such moments of discursive rupture, when certain language or lines of reasoning that I introduced came across as muddled or gauche, that I gained the most insight into the workings of neoliberalism. *Homo oeconomicus* spoke loudly through fundraisers' concern for professional ethics, reputation, and competitive positioning of the nonprofit sector. They could retain a respectable, professional persona in difficult conversations with wealthy donors about issues they deemed ethical, even when there was much at stake. However, many participants seemed uneasy or unprepared to engage as *homo politicus*, that is, to speak in a political register with me. Despite my own interest in the politics of fundraising, I felt similarly awkward about raising certain critical issues. These moments when discursive resources seemed to dry up, when the conversation floundered, signalled that we had departed neoliberal waters and we could no longer assume we held a fully shared, common-sense reality.

References

Brock, D., Raby, R., & Thomas, M. (Eds.). (2012). *Power and Everyday Practices*. Nelson Education.

Burk, P. (2003). *Donor-Centered Fundraising*. Cygnus Applied Research.

Davis, C. W. (2015). *Because Donors Want to Share: A Donor-Centric Approach to Fundraising*. Blunderbuss Books.

van Dijk, T. A. (1993). Principles of Critical Discourse Analysis. *Discourse & Society, 4*(2), 249–283.

Duff, D. G. (2001). Charitable Contributions and the Personal Income Tax: Evaluating the Canadian Credit. In J. Phillips, B. Chapman, & D. Stevens (Eds.), *Between State and Market: Essays on Charities Law and Policy in Canada*. McGill-Queen's University Press.

Foucault, M. (1972 [1969]). *The Archaeology of Knowledge* (A. M. Sheridan Smith, Trans.). Tavistock.

Foucault, M. (1980). *Power/Knowledge: Selected Interviews and Other Writings, 1972–1977*. Vintage.

Glaser, B. G. (1965). The Constant Comparative Method of Qualitative Analysis. *Social Problems, 12*(4), 436–445.

Glaser, B. G., & Strauss, A. L. (1967). *The Discovery of Grounded Theory: Strategies for Qualitative Research*. Aldine Pub. Co.

Hammersley, M. (2010). Reproducing or Constructing? Some Questions about Transcription in Social Research. *Qualitative Research, 10*(5), 553–569. https://doi.org/10.1177/1468794110375230

Healey, R., Bartolini, B., Maehara, P. V., & Williams, C. (2010). *2009–2010 AFP Compensation and Benefits Study*. Retrieved from Arlington, VA.

Hesse-Biber, S. N. (2017). *The Practice of Qualitative Research* (3rd ed.). Sage

M.-B. Raddon, *The Business of Hope*, Palgrave Studies in Third Sector Research, https://doi.org/10.1007/978-3-031-18837-4

Hesse-Biber, S. N., & Leavy, P. (2010). *The Practice of Qualitative Research*. Sage.

Hilborn Civil Sector Press. (n.d.). Hilborn Charity eNEWS. https://www.charityinfo.ca

KCI Philanthropy. (n.d.). Philanthropic Trends. http://kciphilanthropy.com/lang/en/#panel-4-b

Mills, S. (2004 [1997]). *Discourse*. Routledge.

Peacock, R. I. (2007). *Face Time: Relationship Philanthropy: A Resource for Canadian Major Gift Fundraising*. Civil Sector Press.

Roulston, K. (2010). *Reflective Interviewing: A Guide to Theory and Practice*. Sage Publications.

Springer, S. (2016). *The Discourse of Neoliberalism: An Anatomy of a Powerful Idea*. Rowman and Littlefield International.

Index[1]

[1] Note: Page numbers followed by 'n' refer to notes.

M.-B. Raddon, *The Business of Hope*, Palgrave Studies in Third Sector Research, https://doi.org/10.1007/978-3-031-18837-4

The manufacturer's authorised representative in the EU is Springer Nature Customer Service Centre GmbH, Europaplatz 3, 69115 Heidelberg, Germany. If you have any concerns regarding our products, please contact ProductSafety@springernature.com

Printed and bound by CPI Group (UK) Ltd, Croydon, CR0 4YY

01/10/2026

02225879-0005